Dialogues on Moral Education

Dialogues on Moral Education

JOHN WILSON AND BARBARA COWELL

Religious Education Press
Birmingham, Alabama

Library of Congress Cataloging in Publication Data

Wilson, John, 1928–
  Dialogues on moral education.

  Includes index.
  1. Ethics. I. Cowell, Barbara. II. Title.
BJ1012.W538   1983   170   83-4433
ISBN 0-89135-035-7

Religious Education Press, Inc.
1531 Wellington Road
Birmingham, Alabama 35209
10 9 8 7 6 5 4 3 2

Religious Education Press publishes books exclusively in religious education and in areas closely related to religious education. It is committed to enhancing and professionalizing religious education through the publication of serious, significant, and scholarly works.

PUBLISHER TO THE PROFESSION

Contents

First Steps

"Good morning, Cephalus, and why are you sitting there so glumly? Are you not aware that this is a day of rejoicing? It is the anniversary of the battle which we fought against the Persians at Marathon, when we saved the free world."

"That is why I am glum, Socrates. For my own father fought at Marathon, and can you believe that my own son is now in the marketplace taking part in what he calls 'a march of protest' against the celebration of our victory? I am afraid he has fallen in with bad companions."

"Why does he do that, do you think. He is not joking, is he? Or has he decided to be a Persian rather than a Greek?"

The Degeneration of Young People

"By the gods, Socrates, you speak more wisely than you know, for he has begun to dress like a Persian, wearing his

1

hair very long and the most outlandish clothes, so that I really cannot take him into my dining-club and introduce him to my friends, much though this would be to his advantage."

"Come now, Cephalus, surely that is not a very serious matter; it is not the outward appearance that matters in a man, but the soul."

"That is all very well, Socrates, but it is still very worrying, 'for the apparel often proclaims the man,' as one of our poets has it, and I do not feel inclined to trust people who look like that. In any case, he seems to have thrown away all the habits and traditions of his ancestors and has no sense of decency."

"Which ancestors do you mean, Cephalus? Not so long ago, as you once told me, your great-grandfather established his position in a most immoral way, by selling drugs to the innocent natives of these parts and making a great deal of money thereby. And I have heard of other ancestors of yours—like my own, indeed—who founded families by force or fraud. Is it their traditions which your son is throwing away?"

"Of course not, Socrates, all that is in the past. I mean the respectable people of today, like myself and my friends. Do you know, that young man not only says that all war is bad, but also proposes to abolish slavery? I have heard, too, though I can scarcely believe it, that he thinks there is nothing wrong in free-born Athenian women going to parties with men before they are married. But there is something still worse, Socrates."

"Why, what could conceivably be worse than the things you have just mentioned? Unless he not only wears his hair long, but has the barber curl it for him like a woman. Then indeed I can see that you might want to disinherit him, being (I suppose), uncertain as to whether you have a son or a daughter."

"Do not mock me, Socrates. I am not as old-fashioned as you think. It is not so much his particular habits and opinions that worry me, but one big opinion of his that clouds my whole happiness."

"And what is this mighty cloud-opinion? Tell me, and let me see if I can hold a covering over you when it drops rain. For I see, Cephalus, that you are indeed worried and uncertain. Do not imagine that you are like the snowmen which the Hyperboreans make for play, which melt in the rain; surely you are made of sterner stuff than that."

Thinking for Oneself

"Well, Socrates, it seems that he believes that every man should think for himself and form his own opinions about morality and religion and other such things. There, now, keep that rainstorm off if you can. But in my view, it will wash away the whole of our civilization."

"I am not sure if I understand you, Cephalus. How can it be that a man should not think for himself? I mean, I cannot do your thinking for you, nor you for me, any more than I can have your headache, or you mine."

"Don't be silly, Socrates. What he believes is that he should make up his own mind for himself, rather than accepting what our ancestors and other wise men have said."

"I do hope you will not be offended with me, Cephalus, but I am still puzzled as to your meaning. Suppose your son, or any other person—I myself, for instance—considers what has been said by our ancestors and decides to accept it; is not that a case of making up one's mind for oneself? I mean, in this case, I would have made up my mind to accept their authority and to agree with what they say."

"Yes, Socrates, but suppose a person makes up his mind in the other direction, so as to disagree with our ancestors and other authorities?"

"Well, of course, that is possible, Cephalus. But I am still not clear what you mean. Tell me, do you think that young men should consider what has been said by sages and other such people in the past, and perhaps also what is said today?"

"Certainly, they should consider them. How else will they come to believe what is right?"

"Quite true, Cephalus. And by 'consider' do you mean also 'understand'?"

"Of course."

"And you do not just mean, I suppose, that they should be able to repeat their sayings, such as 'Nothing too much' or 'Know yourself' or 'Justice is good.' For one could teach a baby or even a parrot to recite such things. Presumably you think that they must understand their meaning and perhaps come to see why they are true."

"Yes."

"But how are they to do this unless they think for themselves? When they come across any saying, must they not ask themselves 'Is this true?' And must they not then look to see if there are any reasons for or against it?"

"I suppose so."

"Do not grudge me your answer, my dear Cephalus. If you disagree, say so. For I am not one of the gods, you know, who cannot say what is false; indeed I am nobody in particular. I am simply trying to understand, that is all."

Taking Values on Trust

"Well, Socrates, I think that they should take what is said on trust."

"A very good answer, Cephalus, and one which I think I understand. You mean that, if I were to ask you the best way of looking after sheep or growing corn, I should take what you say on trust—since you are a farmer, and I am not skilled in farming—without worrying too much about the reasons for your advice."

"Just so, Socrates."

"But, Cephalus, even though I do not know much about farming, I do know that it is a well-established art, and one which has to be learned. I trust you or any other successful farmer, because I know that you can prove what you say (if I had time to hear the proof) and that any other farmer would say the same. That is, I already know that there are Good reasons for your answer, even if I do not myself know what they are. That is why I trust you. But is it the same with these sages and ancestors you mention?"

"Why should it not be?"

"Well, for one thing, many of them contradict each other; just as there are many religions which say different things and enjoin different kinds of conduct, and some people who do not believe in the gods at all. But, more importantly, I do not think we are dealing with a well-established art here, as farming is. Very often these sages do not give reasons at all, and when they do, they are of different kinds."

The "Good Sages"

"But surely all the good ones say much the same thing, Socrates."

"Which do you call the 'good ones,' Cephalus?"

"I mean the ones who preach decency and order and respect for the gods."

"And what is it that they say, which is 'much the same thing'?"

"Well, they teach us to be respectable and well-behaved, to worship the gods, and to do what is right."

"I must be getting muddled with your answers, Cephalus. It sounded to me as if by 'the good ones' you meant only those sages who said certain things, and then, when I asked what things they recommended, you just repeated yourself. Haven't you just selected certain sages whom you already agree with because of what they say, and decided to call these the 'good ones'? And then you announce that they all say the same thing!—which is hardly surprising, since it is precisely on that basis that you selected them in the first place."

"And why shouldn't I?"

"No reason in the world, my dear friend. But then you mustn't be surprised if other people select different ones. Your son might choose those sages who recommend overthrowing the laws of our ancestors and call those the 'good ones.'"

"Good heavens, Socrates, either you must know my son very well or else you have prophetic powers! That is just what he does do, and I can't understand it."

"Try a little harder, Cephalus. Isn't it the case that, when we call things or people 'good,' we are commending them?"

"Yes, of course."

But Which Sages Are "Good"?

"And we may not always commend the same things as each other. I mean, what the Spartans or Persians call a 'good man' or a 'good king' may not be what you or I would call it."

"True."

"So, then, your son wishes to commend other sages from the ones you wish to commend."

"Yes, Socrates, but he is wrong and I am right."

"Perhaps so. I suppose you mean that there are sound reasons why we ought to commend your sages rather than his?"

"Certainly; for instance, to follow his sages would lead to chaos and. . . ."

"Forgive me for interrupting you, Cephalus, but I am in danger of losing the point, being by nature rather slow-witted and unable to move quickly from one thing to another. I suppose you want to show your son these 'sound reasons,' as you call them, which (in your view) make it wise to follow your sages?"

"Yes, of course."

"So you would like him to consider these reasons, and reflect upon them?"

"Yes."

"And if he claims to have reasons of his own for commending his sages, should these also be considered and discussed?"

"His reasons must be so poor, Socrates, that I do not think they are worth considering."

"But he does not think they are poor, does he? He thinks they are good."

"So he says, but I think mine are good."

"Well, then, are we not in just the same position as before? I mean, your son has a set of sages, and now a set of reasons for listening to his sages, which he calls 'good ones'; and you have different sages and different reasons, which you too call 'good.' So it seems we must give an equal hearing to both sides if we are to make any progress. That is, we must consider these sages and reasons, if we can, from a neutral point of view, in the hope that we can come to learn more and perhaps change our minds."

Shall We Use Force or Argument?

"To be honest, Socrates, I don't much like that idea. I am sure I shall never change my mind—indeed I have no wish to do so. I just want my son to think as I do."

"Then it seems, Cephalus, that we shall have to abandon all discussion and teaching and education and take up sticks and swords. For if we are not going to reason with each other and consider each other's points of view, we can only fight."

"I don't want to do that either, Socrates. As a matter of fact, my son is already bigger and stronger than I am, and I can no longer control his behavior."

"Even if you could, Cephalus, you would not thereby control his opinions. For force does not necessarily make a man change his mind; indeed, it often strengthens his feelings of rebellion. We have seen that in the empire we had under Pericles: We were able to hold them in subjection, but they hated us and thought we were wrong and rebelled as soon as they could."

"Very true, Socrates. But would it have been any better to use reason and discussion?"

"Well, at least we might have tried a bit harder. But if we are going to place our bets on the horse of reason, rather than the horse of violence and force, we must wait until the race is a very long one, and we shall need plenty of patience. Men do not take kindly to reason, though the young would rather be reasoned with than preached at."

"I believe you, Socrates. But how are we to reason with them? What sort of arguments shall we use?"

"That is a difficult matter, Cephalus, but if you are willing to take the first step and address yourself to the problem, perhaps we can discuss it later."

* * *

"Well, Socrates, I have been reflecting about what we said earlier, and I have come to an important decision, which I am sure you will be pleased with."

"And what is that, Cephalus?"

"I felt that I could not, just on my own, undertake to provide reasons and education for all the young men in Athens, so that they would come to believe what was right and true. So I have decided to collect a small group of people who are skilled in such matters and pay them to do it for me—for you know I have money enough and to spare for my own needs."

"A most praiseworthy decision, by Zeus! But tell me, Cephalus, what sort of people are you going to hire, and what do you expect them to do?"

Cephalus Backslides

"I will tell you, Socrates. First, I want to assemble a group of right-minded people, who are thoroughly respectable and have been honored by the state, and who believe in the gods. This will not be difficult, since I know many other older men, besides myself, who are shocked by the young men of today and wish to do something about it. Having done this, we shall try to collect together all the best writings in morality and religion—the 'good sages' we spoke of yesterday, Socrates—and arrange for these to be taught to them by their schoolmasters. Perhaps we may also arrange for them to be publicly declaimed in the marketplace. Further, we shall try to promote the right kinds of music and painting and all the other arts, choosing only such things as are good and respectable, in the hope that all this will encourage our young men to follow the path of virtue."

"Good heavens, Cephalus! I really think I must be losing my memory and had better cut short our conversation and visit the doctor at once."

"Whatever do you mean, Socrates?"

"Well, my dear friend, I must be getting either very forgetful or mentally deranged. For I thought, at the end of our last talk, that you wished to discuss these matters with our young men from a neutral point of view. They have their 'good sages' and you have yours, and did we not say that we were going to examine both and consider the reasons for following either the one or the other?"

"Perhaps we did. But that was not what I had in mind to do, and moreover I have found many other older men who agree with me. We think it important to put a stop to anarchy and permissiveness and all that sort of thing as soon as possible."

Authoritarianism

"If that is what you want, Cephalus, I think you would do better to go to the politicians and persuade them to pass some very severe laws. In Sparta, you know, they do this sort of thing. Young men there are harshly punished if they do not behave in all respects as their elders and betters wish, and they are allowed only to read what their elders think good and forbidden to argue or question anything. Indeed, they are conditioned or indoctrinated to behave in these ways, so that (even if the elders are absent) they themselves are compelled to do what the elders think right. And I believe there have been similar societies among the barbarians, under the rule of Hitler or Stalin or some such person."

"Why do you class me with such dreadful people, Socrates? I do not want to force anybody, but simply to put before them what is good and right."

"And how do you think the young men will react to that, Cephalus?"

"I hope by seeing the virtue of what they read and hear from these good men and coming to practice what they preach."

"Tell me, Cephalus, did you and your older friends bring up your sons to read the works of Homer and the other religious writings which you admire? And did you set them a good example by wearing decent clothes and being clean and tidy and by behaving respectably in general?"

"Certainly we did, Socrates."

"And have your friends' sons, and your own son, followed your example?"

"It seems not."

"So, then, it seems that this method is not enough. Indeed, perhaps it would have been better if you and your friends had dressed like Persians and told your sons that Homer and the other 'good sages' were not good at all, but bad; then perhaps your sons would have reacted against your teaching, and come to believe in Homer and the others. For it seems that the young follow a principle propounded by some sage—I forgot whom—that 'every action has an equal and opposite reaction.'"

"It seems so, indeed. For I have often noticed, Socrates, that, not only in families, but in whole cities people swing violently from one side to the other, like the pendulum of a clock. Monarchy is followed by extreme democracy, and that again by another monarchy or dictatorship; just as with the fashions in women's clothes, where it seems that there is always a reaction against what has gone before."

"Very true, Cephalus. But I have a proposition to make to you."

"What is that?"

"Well, we two old men have been sitting here talking about how the young are likely to receive your plans. But why do we not ask your son, whom I observed reading in the portico just outside?"

"If you wish, Socrates. But I must warn you that my son, Antiphon, is not a calm and civilized disputant, as you and I are. He is indeed well-named, since he is 'anti' everything, or so it appears to me."

"Never mind, Cephalus, let me call him. Antiphon! My dear young friend do come in and enlighten us old folk, for we were discussing something about which you have expert knowledge."

"Me? You're kidding. Father doesn't think I know anything about anything—except where to find a cheap girlfriend."

"A very useful piece of knowledge too, Antiphon. But have you heard what your father proposed to do?"

"Something boring, I expect."

Antiphon Dislikes the "Good Sages"

"That is what we want your opinion about, my dear fellow. He proposes to collect together all the 'good sages,' as he calls them—the men of religion, like Homer and the rest—and ensure that they are taught to young people throughout the city, so that the young will come to follow the path of true virtue."

"Who says that such people can show us 'true virtue'? And how do we know they are really 'good' sages, anyway?"

"Well, that is a question about which Cephalus has not yet enlightened us. But tell me, how would you react to such a proposal?"

"I'll tell *you,* Socrates, for you've always been a good friend to me and listened to what I've had to say. My father just thinks I'm bad and stupid, and he is so old-fashioned that I can't take him seriously."

"Tell me, Antiphon, are you interested in the truth?"

"What do you mean?"

"Well, you are a grown man now, and—so I have always believed—an intelligent one. So that I do not really understand your attitude to your father. I mean, if you are interested in what is true and right, presumably you will listen to anyone who has something useful to say. It would not matter, would it, if true words came from the mouth of a goat or a mule?"

"No."

Antiphon Encouraged to Reason

"And perhaps your father is no worse than those animals. I know that you do not like the clothes he wears and the company he keeps—any more than he likes yours—but I have never understood what that has to do with it. For myself, I am afraid I am not very observant; I can see now that your hair and clothes and way of talking are not like my own, but I won't remember this for very long. And I enjoy talking to you, not because you wear certain clothes or are 'modern'—how could that matter?—but because you seem to be interested in learning about what is true, as I am."

"Yes, Socrates, but you must admit that it is very aggravating when a person behaves like my father here, always saying how wrong young people are today and criticizing them in all sorts of ways."

"Really, Antiphon? I have always found the opposite. For, though I am unobservant, I know well enough that many people seem to dislike me and want to criticize me and my views, and these are just the people I cultivate. After all, if you wished to test the strength and soundness of the floor of a house, you would not just pat it gently, would you?"

"What do you mean?"

"Surely you would jump on it as hard as possible, to see if it would stand up to attack. So too I welcome the strongest criticism of what I say, to see if the floor of my opinion is solid."

"Very well, Socrates, but then my father ought to do the same. I will listen to his criticism, if he will listen to mine."

"Well, now Cephalus, you have sat silently by for a space; how do you feel about this?"

A Family Argument

"I have kept quiet, Socrates, for when I speak on such matters Antiphon usually jumps down my throat."

"Really, father! How can you say that, when it is always you who are attacking me?"

"Nonsense, boy! I may have voiced a few criticisms. . . ."

"A few criticisms! Let me tell you, you've never. . . ."

At this point I saw Cephalus and Antiphon becoming very angry and forgetting that I was there; so, rather than interfere with a family discussion, I decided that I should slip quietly away. I had just got as far as the door when Cephalus noticed me and said:

"Socrates! Where are you going?"

"Well, my dear fellow, I thought that Antiphon and you were considering a family business and would rather not have strangers like myself present. So I decided to disappear."

"What a bad host you must think me, Socrates! We do not treat guests like that in this house. I am afraid I let my feelings carry me away."

"There, Antiphon, do you hear that? It cannot be true, as you say, that your father is always criticizing you, for now he has criticized himself."

"Yes, Socrates, and rightly."

"And do you have no criticisms to offer?"

"I suppose so, Socrates. My own feelings get the better of me at times."

"There, Cephalus! Now, shall I tell you what I think, or will you both be offended and throw me out of the house?"

"No, do tell us, of course. For I at least feel a little ashamed of myself and would welcome your criticism."

"I have nothing harsh to say, but the opposite. For it seems to me, Cephalus and Antiphon, that you are both pretending or acting a part, as in the comedies of Aristophanes. You pretend to quarrel and hate each other and use angry words, but really you behave like this because you love each other and neither of you can bear the other to be different and separate from himself. For otherwise, if you really hated or were indifferent to each other you would not bother to talk together at all, but would go your separate ways."

"It may be so, Socrates. But now, to seal our friendship, I propose to bring down a jar of that Chian wine, which Antiphon has always liked, and which we can drink together."

"The old Chian, father? I thought it was all finished."

"Well, my boy, I was saving it for your birthday; I was going to give it to you then and let you take it away and drink it with your friends, since you seem to prefer their company to mine. Perhaps that is what you would rather do?"

"What do you say to that, Antiphon?"

"I say that my father is the best of all fathers and that I would much prefer to drink it with him here and now."

At this I saw Cephalus look happier than he had done for some time, and after we had drunk together a little they began to discuss the farms which Cephalus owned, and whether Antiphon would be interested in running them. So I excused myself, with a promise to return and take up the discussion again.

*   *   *

Next day I returned to find Cephalus and Antiphon having an animated but amicable discussion, and as soon as I came in Antiphon jumped up and said:

"Socrates. Just the man we need! He will settle our disputes for us, won't he, father?"

"Yes, my boy, I am sure he will, won't you, Socrates?"

There Are No Quick "Answers" in Philosophy

"My dear Cephalus and Antiphon, you do me too much honor. I am not the Delphic oracle, you know."

"But you are the wisest man we know, so we are prepared to believe what you tell us—at least I am, and I expect Antiphon will too. So do tell us the answer."

"I am absolutely amazed, my friends; indeed I am not sure if I understand you. Is it some technical point about stone or sculpture that you are disputing—I might be able to help you there, since I am trained as a stonemason—or what?"

"Of course not, Socrates. Antiphon and I were arguing about what we discussed before; about the basis of morality and religion, and what to teach the young. I was maintaining that morality depended on a divine law which existed in nature, and Antiphon claimed that this was not so, but that each person had to decide for himself."

"I should not be surprised if you were both right. But how can I 'tell you the answer,' as you call it?"

"Why, by telling us which view is correct. You can do that, can't you?"

"It seems to me, Cephalus, that you and your son are men of extremes, and not the moderates I took you for. Why, only yesterday you were quarreling in front of me and behaved as if I did not exist, and today you seem to look on me as possessing some divine wisdom, so that you are willing to entrust the dispute to me as to some god or other."

"Well, but can you not help us, Socrates?"

"I will give all the help I can, naturally. But tell me, do

you think morality a smaller thing than painting or music?"

"No, but why do you ask?"

"Suppose I went to a painter, like Polygnotus, and asked him to teach me how to paint well. Do you think he could 'tell me the answer' quickly?"

"No, for it takes many years to learn to paint well."

Nor in Morality

"And yet he could do certain things quickly. For instance, I could ask him 'What is a good painter?' and he could reply 'Someone who paints beautiful pictures'; but that would not be very helpful. Or again, I could take a brush in my hand and get him to guide my hand for me, so that the lines and strokes were correct, or perhaps he could divide up the spaces for me beforehand and give me instructions, like 'Color that part blue,' 'Put some red here,' and so on. All that could be done fairly easily, could it not?"

"Certainly, Socrates, but that in itself would not make you good at painting, nor better able to understand what good painting was. For it would really be Polygnotus, not you, who was doing all the work."

"It is just the same with morality and the good life, Cephalus. Even if I were to give you quick answers, such as 'Do what Homer says,' or 'Obey the sayings of Solon,' or even if I stood over you at each moment of the day and issued instructions, that would not make you a good man. You would have to learn to understand things for yourself, would you not?"

"I suppose so."

"And it is even more difficult than that. For with painting and music, and still more obviously with the arts and sciences (like farming and masonry), we already know what is to count as 'good'; we know what a good farm is, and perhaps what a good painting or piece of music is. So we would not disagree much about the end product and could confine our discussion to ways and means. But when we are thinking of the good life, or the basis of morality, we do not already have this agreement, do we? For if we did, I imagine that philosophers and moralists would not keep arguing with each other as they do now. There are many different sorts of lives advocated by different people, all of them worth listening to."

"There you are, father! I told you Socrates would agree with me! It is just a matter of taste or opinion what is good and bad; there is no question of a 'divine law' or anything of that kind."

Morality Not a Matter of Taste

"I did not say that, Antiphon. I said that all the opinions were worth listening to, but not because they were all right—indeed, how could that be so, since they contradict each other? I simply thought that, if we listened critically to them, we might come to see whether there were good reasons for believing some rather than others."

"There you are, Antiphon! Socrates thinks, as I do, that there is one right answer, one divine law for all men, which is given us by the gods; it is not a matter of taste or opinion at all."

Nor of "Divine Law" in Any Simple Sense

"I did not say that either, Cephalus. For there are many things which are not just matters of taste or opinion, and yet I do not think you would want to call all these 'divine law.' For instance, it is right to make certain moves in a game of draughts, and not other moves, or to pump the bilgewater from a ship before setting sail, or to use certain words if you want to convey something and not other words. But if all these things are laid down by the gods, they must indeed be very busy. Which god is it, for instance, that has laid down the law about the right moves to make in draughts? I wish he would lay it down more clearly, and then I would not lose so often."

"I was not speaking of such things, Socrates, but of high and important matters, such as justice and truthfulness and decent behavior."

"Ah, I see. Well, I have a suggestion to make."

"What?"

"Since you have chosen me as an arbitrator, I suggest that you should each in turn set out your views, like competing designs for the construction of a new temple. For I am not yet clear exactly what each of you thinks—and it may even be that you yourselves are not wholly clear, until you set everything out in full. So do not worry about monopolizing the conversation, for the time being, but sketch out your designs in turn. How do you like that idea?"

"Very well, Socrates, who is to begin?"

"Perhaps you would begin, Cephalus, and Antiphon afterwards."

Cephalus on "Divine Law"

"Well, then, Socrates, since you have asked me, I will speak. I cannot pretend to be eloquent, or to dress up my views in poetical and glorious clothes, since I am no poet. In any case, it seems to me that what I have to say is obvious enough. That is why, perhaps, I sometimes get angry with Antiphon here and others. The truth is so obvious, that they must surely be deliberately blinding themselves or trying to annoy me.

"First, then, I think that there is a god, or gods, who control the world and all that is in it. This is clear enough from what we see in nature. We do not see disorder and chaos, but order and harmony. Crops grow at their appointed seasons, the day and night (and the months and years) follow each other in due order; not only the animals but plants and even rivers and rocks all obey natural laws relating to their own kind. Now it is surely the case that man can be no exception to this rule; there must be a natural or divine law for him also.

"Second, Socrates, it seems to me that there cannot in the nature of things be any other basis for morality. For what secure basis could we find in human reason, or in human feelings? Both are weak and fallible, but only the gods are immortal and infallible. What is true and right cannot depend on man's will and beliefs alone; if that were so, we could make true and right whatever we wanted to make. It must depend on the will of God.

"Third, is it not true that we sense this will within our own hearts, whenever we attend to them closely? We know well enough, by our own consciences, what is right and wrong—that is, what accords with the divine law and what does not. There are very few men who do not have a sense of shame about sexual matters, for instance, not to mention robbery and murder and other such things. We may try to deny this knowledge—this natural light, so to speak, which illuminates every one of us, but it is still there. How could it exist if it were not the gift of the gods?

"Finally, Socrates—for I will be as brief as I can—look at

what happens if all this is denied. As the poet says, 'things fall apart,' and 'mere anarchy is loosed upon the world.' When religious belief fails, chaos ensues; every man is for himself, and there is an end to law and order—unless perhaps some tyrant cashes in on the situation, like the Hitler you spoke of. In a word, Socrates, man is not the measure of all things, as some sophist would have us believe. Over man are set the gods and the divine law; to them we are as children—too often, I fear, disobedient children. And that is all I will say for the present."

"Well, then, Antiphon, let us see your design."

Antiphon Denies It All

"Mine is simpler still, Socrates, than my father's. For I completely deny almost everything he has said. I do not believe in the gods; even if I did, I do not see why we should obey them or their 'divine law.' Things in nature— I mean the animals and plants and so on that my father mentions—may obey laws, I suppose, but human beings have free will and are not like the senseless beasts. They must decide what is best for themselves.

"As to father's point about the weakness of human reasons and feeling, I could perhaps agree, but surely it is cowardly to give up just because one is weak? Much of the weakness, in my opinion, comes from what he regards as a source of strength. He calls it 'conscience,' but I think it is simply the residue of primitive feelings which were drummed into us as young children—we would be better off without them, and then perhaps we would be stronger to decide for ourselves what to do.

"In short, Socrates, I see no alternative but to strip away all the silly conventions and false moralities with which our fathers, and their fathers before them, have saddled and swathed us. They are obviously irrational and have handicapped the young for too long. A man must act as he feels; there is no guide except what each of us wants to do. Indeed, the young men of my company have a watchword, which may sound strange to you; we call it 'doing your own thing,' to show that no one else has any right to lay down the law about what is good and bad. We are not children, as my father says; we are men, and must be free."

After both of them had spoken, I was wondering how best to proceed with the argument, when suddenly Cephalus said:

"Antiphon, do you know what I think?"

"No, what?"

Neither Has a Properly Considered Opinion

"Well, it strikes me that we are both playing the same game as before, only on a grander and more magnificent board."

"How do you mean?"

"Until recently we had been quarreling, had we not? And I suppose it was a typical quarrel between father and son. I wanted to insist on my authority as a father and the values and behavior that went with it, and you wanted to reject and deny it. Isn't that so?"

"Yes."

"But now, though we are not quarreling any more, are we not really saying the same sort of thing, only in a more high-minded way? I mean, I have been talking about the gods, who are like fathers, and the values and divine law which I believe in, and you have been talking like a son, who is not willing to accept them (even if they exist)."

"Yes, I see what you mean. It is true that I do not like the idea of there being any gods to tell us what to do. I want to assert myself and claim my rights as a free-thinking adult. Is that right, Socrates?"

"Well, Antiphon, since you have said so, I agree. Perhaps it is worth noting that human beings do this very often; they take their own personal feelings, concerned with their families or friends, and elevate them into philosophical theories. This is something we have always to beware of, though it is very difficult to escape."

But Rather a Fantasy

"But then is is very alarming, Socrates. For I thought just now that I had a strong belief in what I was saying; yet it turns out that I may not really believe it, as a man believes that two and two are four, but rather cling to it as a man may cling to a piece of wood when he is drowning, or to a spear when he is fighting. It is more like a kind of picture or fantasy that I have in my mind, to which I am very strongly attached. Whether it is true or not, I am more uncertain than I was before."

"How about you, Cephalus?"

"I feel much the same, Socrates. Obviously, I have a lot of emotion invested in my picture. But that does not mean, does it, that the matter is not worth pursuing? Even if we are both prejudiced and think as we do because of our emotions, there is presumably still something that we *ought* to think? Do I make myself clear?"

"Very clear, Cephalus, and I agree with you. For a man may have dreams or fantasies about, say, what Sparta is like, or what happened during the Persian Wars; yet, there is still a real Sparta and a true account of the Persian Wars.

So that we need not give up hope. But we must be on our guard, because these dreams come into our heads very often, and we do not notice them; it is then that we become violent or fearful and forget about the truth."

"Well, Socrates, I hope you will help us in this, at any rate, even if you cannot 'tell us the answer.' Perhaps tomorrow we shall be able to make better progress."

CHAPTER 2

Morals and Religion

On the following day I arrived early, for I was sure that the conversation would go on for some considerable time, and I happened to find Cephalus making sacrifices and praying to the gods. When he had finished, I said:

"Now I perceive, Cephalus, that your words are backed by deeds. For you were saying yesterday, were you not, that our lives ought to be lived in accordance with the will of the gods and the divine law, and I imagine that you were trying to follow your own advice just now."

"Yes, Socrates. I was trying to find out what is the divine will with regard to my wife and children. For I am getting old and must make many decisions which will affect their future."

Cephalus Claims to Know the "Divine Law"

"Tell me, Cephalus, in what way exactly do you find out what the divine will is? Do you watch for the flight of birds or other such omens, or what?"

"Certainly not; I do not hold with such mumbo-jumbo. That is superstition, Socrates, and not true religion at all."

"What do you do, then? I mean, how do you tell whether something is the voice of God, or part of the divine law, or whether it is just an idle fancy of your own?"

"It is obvious to any decent citizen, Socrates."

"Is it, indeed? I daresay you are right, yet I am still puzzled. For consider: There are many religions, such as those of the Jews and the Egyptians, and there are some among the barbarians who worship stranger gods—even their own leaders, like that Hitler and Stalin we mentioned before. I suppose, indeed, that there must be as many religions and gods as men have fancies and desires; perhaps the two are connected in some way. But anyhow, you are not saying that all these religions are right at once, are you?"

"Of course not. Some of them are true and spiritual religions; others are little better than superstition."

"And how do you tell the 'true and spiritual religions,' as you call them?"

"Very easily, Socrates. If their preachers and followers and sacred writings teach us what we know to be right and good and inspiring, then they are good and spiritual religions. If not, then they are bad."

But Argues in a Circle

"Perhaps I had better go to that doctor after all, Cephalus, for it sounded as if you were saying something which you could not possibly mean—so I suppose my memory is at fault. Please assist me. Over the past day or so we have been discussing, haven't we, how to determine the proper life for man?"

"We have."

"And the question arose, what sort of morality was to count as 'good,' didn't it?"

"Yes."

"And you said that we should adopt the morality laid down by your 'good sages,' as you called them?"

"I did."

"Would you say your 'good sages' were associated with what you call the 'true and spiritual religions,' Cephalus?"

"Of course; that is exactly what I meant."

"Then something has gone wrong somewhere, for when I asked just now how one was to identify the 'true and spiritual religions,' you said (in effect) that it depended on whether a religion advocated the right sort of morality—as if you already knew which was the right sort of morality from some other source."

"My head is spinning, Socrates. Can you not make it simpler for me?"

"Well, Cephalus, let me tell you of an argument I had the other day with a Jew. The Jews have a sacred book, you know, which they call the Bible. I asked this man why he believed in his God. 'Because it says so in the Bible,' he replied. 'But why do you believe the Bible?' I asked him. 'Because it is the word of God,' he said. At this point I bade him good day, because I thought that he must be joking with me."

"And have I done something of that kind?"

"Well a malicious person might think so, Cephalus. He might say: 'Cephalus, I think you must be joking with poor old Socrates here. For when he asked you what was the right morality, you told him it was what the "good sages" or "true religions" recommended. And, when he asked you how you identified the "good sages" and "true religions," you told him that it was those who recommended the right morality. No wonder he feels that he has lost his memory; you have made a proper fool of him, and no mistake.' Might he not say something like that?"

"Well, Socrates, it seems that I have made some kind of mistake. We must, I suppose, find some other way to identify both what the right morality is and which are the good sages; either that, or I must make up my mind which one of the two comes first, and which is dependent upon it."

"I like your first suggestion better. But let me see if I understand what you think about the gods, Cephalus. Or rather, let me put some questions to your son Antiphon, who I see coming, since it may be that you are getting tired of my talk."

"Not at all, Socrates, but do as you think best."

"Antiphon, I want you to help me and Cephalus by making a great effort of imagination. Will you do that?"

"I will try."

Why Should We Obey the "Divine Law"?

"Well, then, let us suppose that all the beliefs of Cephalus about the gods and the divine law are true. That is, let us suppose that some god created this world and everything in it and has laid down laws, not only for animals and plants and the like, but also for human beings, and he intended us to follow those laws. Let us suppose further, if you will grant this for the time being, that we know what these laws are—whether from some prophet or sacred book, or perhaps we can imagine them written in enormous letters of fire, high up in the sky, or what you will. Now, if all that were so, would we not be right to obey them?"

"Not necessarily, Socrates."

"What, Antiphon! Will you grant all that, and not grant what seems to be the obvious conclusion?"

"Obvious to you and Cephalus, perhaps, but not to me."

"What have we missed, then?"

"Well, Socrates, suppose you were an animal on our farm. Then your whole world would have been created, in effect, by the farmers, and we would have laid down laws for you to follow, along with the other animals. And you might know what those laws were (assuming you could read). But it would not always follow, would it, that you ought to obey them? I mean, for instance, we farmers might be making the laws for our own benefit, and not for yours; or else perhaps we have your interest at heart, but make mistakes and set up the wrong laws sometimes."

"I suppose so, Antiphon. But do you liken the gods to farmers?"

"My point is, Socrates, that it is not a good reason for obeying someone just because he is very powerful, or has created the conditions under which we live. If we were assured that he was well-disposed toward us, and wiser than we, then we might agree to fall in with his advice, but that would not be like obeying a tyrant just because of his power—it would be more like accepting the advice of a friend. In any case, Socrates, it is we who have to make the initial judgment; I mean, it is we who have to decide whether the person (be he a god, or a tyrant, or a farmer) is giving us good advice."

"And can't we decide that?"

Antiphon Thinks Morals Are Arbitrary

"Certainly we can, but then we must know what counts as 'good advice' from some other source, not just from what the gods tell us; otherwise we will be arguing in a circle."

"I seem to recognize that circle already, Antiphon; Cephalus and I were discussing it just before you came in. But what do you propose that we should do in order to escape from it?"

"I see no escape, and that is why I think each man just chooses his own morality arbitrarily and to suit himself, so that there is no question of any law, divine or otherwise."

"Well, let us examine what you have just said. We call a decision 'arbitrary,' do we not, when there is no reason for it one way or the other?"

"We do."

"And is that what you think happens with morality?"

"Yes."

"Tell me, Antiphon, you speak the Greek language fairly well, do you not?"

"Of course, since I am Greek. But what has that to do with anything?"

"Are there words in Greek such as 'right,' 'wrong,' 'good,' 'bad,' 'ought,' and the like?"

"You really are silly, Socrates; of course there are, since you have just pronounced them."

"And these words have some meaning, do they not?"

"Certainly."

"And what do you think they mean? For instance, if a man calls something 'good' or says that he 'ought' to do it, do you think he is just commending that thing arbitrarily (as you call it), or just saying 'I like it,' or something of that kind?"

"Probably."

But Perhaps There Are Reasons for Morality

"I do not think that can be quite right, Antiphon, or at least not the whole story. For there are many things which we do not like, but which (we say) are 'good' for us, such as unpleasant medicines. Moreover, if somebody says that something is good, it would be quite natural for me to ask him why he thinks it is good, and very often he can give me some kind of a reason in reply. This is obvious enough when we talk of good knives, and good horses, and the like, and I do not see why it should not be the same with good men and good lives."

"But what sort of reasons are there to be given in this case, Socrates? For we are not now going to fall back on my father's views, according to which we say that a good life or morality is what 'good sages' recommend and define 'good sages' as those who recommend good morality—that gets us nowhere."

"Would you be content, then, with something along the lines which you yourself were taking in your long speech yesterday? I mean, when you were talking about being strong and free, not hampered by outworn conventions, and so on. Is that the right sort of reason to use?"

"I am not sure now, Socrates. I want to be strong and free, but I would not quite like to say that it is morally right or good; that seems to take all the joy out of it somehow."

"Forgive me for talking like a father, Antiphon, but do you not perhaps feel that any kind of reason for choosing one way to live rather than another would be a sort of chain round your feet, so to speak? As if following reason and truth were somehow like obeying the orders of a tyrant?"

"Well, there may be something in what you say, Socrates. Certainly I have often been fed up with schoolmasters and other people telling me to 'be reasonable' or 'be sensible'—by which they usually meant that I should do as they wanted."

"But you are grown up now, Antiphon, and I think you do yourself an injustice. For consider: Do you really think there are no good reasons for being strong and free, as you just said? Do you think it is just a whim of yours, so that someone who wanted to be weak and a slave—if he had that whim—would be just as sensible?"

Here Antiphon took a little time to consider, but Cephalus broke in and said:

Cephalus Sees Some Reasons

"I have been fretting all this while, Socrates, because I am still inclined to believe that my gods and the divine law have something to do with it. But now that you and Antiphon are arguing like those who are sometimes called 'humanists,' who leave out the divine altogether, I must at least see that human justice is done to the argument—and to Antiphon himself. So may I ask him some questions for a change?"

"Of course, Cephalus; he is your son, after all."

"Well, then, Antiphon—I will not call you 'my boy,' for we are speaking now as equals in the argument—I think that what you describe as the 'strong' and the 'free' can easily be defended. Tell me, have I restricted your freedom in the past?"

"Yes, father—or Cephalus, I should say."

"And made you feel weak and small, I expect?"

"Sometimes, certainly."

"So now you want to be strong and free, in order to escape from my tyranny?"

"Well, I would not want to put it like that."

"Do not spare my feelings, Antiphon, and if you are feeling well-disposed toward me now, try to remember the way you have felt on other occasions. It is true, isn't it, that you often wished yourself bigger than I and free from my power as a father?"

"Yes, I suppose so."

"Very natural, too. I felt just the same when I was young. But now tell me—for this is the question I really wanted to ask—is it only for that reason that a young man should want to be strong and free? I mean this; when I die, I shall no longer be able to control or influence you at all—unless it is from beyond the grave, like Agamemnon in Aeschylus' play. But would you then wish to be weak and a slave, or be indifferent about it?"

"No, of course not."

"Then must there not be some other reason, independent of you and me, why strength and freedom are good things for men?"

"I suppose so."

"But surely this reason is very obvious, Antiphon—much more obvious than those gods and sages of mine whom I mentioned earlier. I am surprised that you do not see it. The reason is that whatever a man wants or desires or tries to do or be he will need strength and freedom as allies, just as he will need health, and the use of his limbs, and various other things."

"It seems so."

"Well, Socrates, are you not proud of me both as a pupil

and as a father? I have not only assisted the argument, but I have shown that Antiphon's views can readily be defended. I think I shall take to philosophy in my old age."

"I am glad to hear you say that, Cephalus, for, though we have made some progress, there is a long way to go in the discussion. We have not yet clarified what these reasons are which may form the basis for morality and whether we are entitled to speak of them as 'divine law' or in other terms. And we have not even begun to discuss how to teach the young men of the city to become better. But still, perhaps that is enough for one day."

"No, Socrates; do let us continue after luncheon, for sometimes, if we abandon a topic overnight, it sinks below the surface of the soul and is forgotten, as, just now, I forgot what I had said the day before."

"Very well; after lunch, then."

*   *   *

When we had finished luncheon, I noticed that Antiphon was looking somewhat troubled. So I offered to pour him some wine and said to him:

"Drink up, Antiphon! And cheer up, too! Would you prefer to abandon our discussion for the day? It is true, as they say, that too much philosophy at once is an intolerable thing—just like a surfeit of wine, or truffles, or any other rich food."

Obeying Authorities Is No Solution

"It is not a surfeit that I suffer from, but a lack, Socrates; or so it seems to me. For now that I understand a little better what my father Cephalus thinks about the gods and the 'good sages,' I am troubled on his behalf."

"How do you mean?"

"Well, I will try to explain. Hitherto I had thought that all this talk of gods and sages and other such was an invention of old men and the rulers of states who were trying to pretend that their authority came from a divine source, in order that they might continue to rule over their sons and citizens without trouble. There is a wise barbarian, one Marx, who puts all this better than I can and who says that 'religion is the opium of the people'—opium being, I understand, a kind of barbarian drug which puts one is a state of somnolence. The idea is that the rich men and rulers give the people religion in order to keep them quiet and obedient."

"But now I see that it is a deeper thing than that. For the old men and rulers themselves believe this; they have, as it were, swallowed their own drug. They are so weak and fearful that they cannot live without obedience to another, and since they have no rulers over them they must imagine a set of divine rulers—gods and sages and heroes and other such figures—who will tell them what to do with their lives. They do not want to be free, as I do; they want to be slaves of the gods, which is indeed the most piteous kind of slavery, since they are subjected to something of their own invention and not real at all."

"What do you think of that, Cephalus?"

"Well, Socrates, of course I admit that my religion is a great comfort to me; indeed, I do not know how I could live without it. As I see it, a man must have something to believe in and some great example to admire and live up to; without this he will fall to pieces. And today, not only do the young men not believe in the gods, but there are very few heroes and great men for them to admire—men like Achilles and Odysseus and Solon and other such."

"You see, Socrates? It is just as I said. My father admits, in effect, that he *needs* to believe in such things. He does not say they are true, or produce evidence and reasons for them; he says only that to believe in them is comforting and useful."

"And perhaps it is, Antiphon, for when men are older and weaker and nearer to death, as your father and I are, it is very helpful to have some belief of this kind. But tell me, Cephalus, are you still inclined to look to these gods and sages for a basis for morality, or do you prefer to search for reasons elsewhere? Yesterday, when you were questioning Antiphon about the strong and the free, it seemed to me that you were searching elsewhere, but I am not sure."

"I am not sure myself, Socrates."

"Goodness" Not a Single Quality

"Well, perhaps I can help you. It may be, you know, that we are behaving like the mad Thracian in the story."

"What story is that?"

"It seems that this Thracian was anxious to preserve his health, and had heard that there was a certain 'health food,' as it is called, sold in the shops. So he thought that, if only he could buy some food of this kind, he would not need to bother about other foodstuffs, or about his diet in general, but would be able to get all the health he wanted from this one food alone. But when he went to the shops, all he could find were a number of ordinary foods—bread and oranges and onions and so on—and no single 'health food' at all."

"But did he not realize, Socrates, that it is just these different foods which bring health?"

"Apparently not. He seems to have thought that there must somehow be one food, like the nectar or ambrosia of the gods (or like mother's milk for the infant), which would do everything for him at once. The doctors and shop-owners tried to explain to him, but he would not listen; he went about wailing 'Alas! There is nothing that can give me health! We are all doomed!' and so on and so forth."

"But how do you apply this to our case?"

"Well, Cephalus, perhaps we are like this Thracian in that we too may be seeking some one thing, which we call 'the basis of morality'; but perhaps there are a number of different things, which can satisfy us well enough once we understand better. Just now we were wondering whether to pursue ordinary human reasons for such a basis, or whether to bring in divine aid. But perhaps these two things are like two different foods, which have their own special function for the body's health."

"Go on."

Incentives and Justifications

"I do not want to give you a lecture, Cephalus, but I can offer you another parable. The other day I met a man who was building a bridge for himself. He had been working all day making the necessary measurements and laying the foundations and so on and was rather tired, and as I passed, he said, 'Oh, Socrates! Why in the world should I bother to do all this work? It is so complicated and difficult!' Now, I have rather a simple, literal mind so I answered him literally and said, 'My friend, why do you ask me for reasons? You know more about bridge-building than I do. I imagine that, in order to get a good bridge, you have to measure and plan as you are doing. There must be good reasons which justify your having to take care and thought, which you yourself know.' 'But, Socrates,' he replied, 'it is so laborious that I feel inclined to give it up altogether. I really don't want to make the effort.' 'I apologize for misunderstanding you,' I said. 'At first I thought you wanted good *reasons* for your actions— that you wanted to know what made it rational for you to measure this piece of land, and shape that stone, and so on, and this puzzled me, for you know such reasons better than I. But now I see that you are seeking, not reasons, but some sort of inspiration or incentive, something that will encourage you to continue the work or compel you to do it. Mind you, I do not know that I can help you much there either. But perhaps you could imagine yourself how nice it will be when your bridge is finished; or perhaps you could ask your friends to come here, so that you would be ashamed if you had nothing to show them; or perhaps you have a nagging wife, who will spur you on; or you may believe that the bridge has been ordered by the gods, who will be angry if you do not finish it.' And so we parted."

Antiphon here chipped in with a smile: "What a cunning old fox you have invited into our house, father! Socrates never says anything in his own person, but either gets us to admit it for ourselves, or else he tells us parables. What he is saying now is this: that we are stupid to talk of 'the basis of morality,' as a thing we can seek for: First, we can seek for reasons or justifications for living in one way rather than another, and that is one thing; second, we can try to find, not a reason, but some sort of incentive or power which will actually help us or make us follow these reasons, and that is quite a different thing. But why he does not come right out and say this for himself, I cannot understand."

"Well, Antiphon, you have said it for me, and much more clearly than I could, I'm sure. It is a kind of modesty, you know, or else perhaps pure laziness, which makes me proceed in the way I do, for who am I to say what you and Cephalus should think? And if someone younger and more energetic, like yourself, can set out the truth for me, I am only too glad."

"All right, Socrates, have it your way. But now, how shall we proceed? Shall we consider the first of these two things—the reasons or justifications for morality—or the second, that is, the incentive or inspiration? For I suppose we need both."

"I will leave it to Cephalus' decision, since it is his house we are in."

"Well, Socrates, I am proud of the way in which my son Antiphon has clarified the matters that lie before us, but I am nonetheless worried about this choice. For I must admit that, like the Thracian, I would like to have both at once—I mean, both the reasons and the incentive. That is why, perhaps, it is so convenient to believe in the gods and a divine law, for God seems, at least, to provide me with both a reason for morality and an incentive for following it."

Different Sorts of Reasons

"I sympathize with you, Cephalus. In fact, although Antiphon here is so clear, I am still perplexed about these two things, so I would like to seek some more information from him. May I do that, Antiphon?"

"Of course."

"Well, then, you remember that when you were younger you would often do something because your father said so?"

"Naturally."

"But what should I mean by 'because' here? Was your father saying so a reason for your doing it, or just an incentive?"

"I am not sure, Socrates."

"Neither am I, Antiphon. Let us look at it this way. When your father said, for example, 'Go to bed, Antiphon' or 'Put down that knife,' what did you say to yourself? Did you say, 'Yes, I am tired, so I ought to go to bed' or 'Yes, the knife is dangerous, so I ought to put it down'? That would be a good reason, I suppose."

"Sometimes, Socrates, but not often, I think. More commonly I said to myself something like 'I must do what father says, because—' well, Socrates, I do not quite know because of what; it just seemed to me that I ought to do what he said. That does not look like a reason at all, does it?"

"No, I agree; it seems more as if you were being driven like a beast (with respect to you, Cephalus); or as when a man shouts at us fiercely, we naturally recoil and turn away, at least to begin with. But surely that is not the whole story. Did you never say to yourself something like, 'I must do what father says, because otherwise he will be angry and I will be punished'?"

"Yes, often."

"But now this is a reason, isn't it? Only a different sort of reason, not concerned with why it is sensible for anyone to go to bed or put down the knife, but concerned with your own immediate advantage in respect of what your father might do."

"I suppose it is a reason."

"Is it a good reason, or not?"

"Well, in a way it is a very good reason, Socrates. After all, what better reason could a man have than to avoid being punished and hurt?"

"Yes, but is it a good reason for going to bed or putting down the knife? Or is it just a good reason for doing what your father says—whether it be going to bed, or not going to bed, or doing anything else that he tells you to?"

"It is very difficult to say, Socrates."

"I agree with you. But perhaps at least we could say this, that there seem to be two different chains of thought here—what the young Aristotle would call 'syllogisms,' I believe. One is, 'Do what your father says, to avoid punishment; father says this, therefore do this.' Another is, 'Do what is beneficial to your mind and body; sleep is beneficial for you now, therefore go to bed' (and the same with putting down the knife). Are these not different?"

"They are."

"Now does it not seem to you that, though the first chain of thought is often more efficient as an incentive, the second is in a way prior to it?"

"How so?"

"I mean that, if the second were not valid, neither your father nor anyone else would have any justification for employing the first."

"I am not sure if I follow you."

Good Reasons in Themselves

"Well, Antiphon, if there were not good reasons in their own right, so to speak, for going to bed when you are tired, or putting down knives that may cut you, there would be no sense in fathers or other people using other reasons to get you to do these things."

"No, there would be no sense at all. And yet they often do."

"Perhaps so, Antiphon, but doesn't this show us that we must seek for the good reasons in themselves, as perhaps we may call them, before anything else? And then, having established these, we can see how the land lies as regards any other reasons, or incentives, or whatever they may be."

"Certainly, but I am still not clear whether they are reasons or just incentives. I thought that I was, after you had told us the parable about the bridge-builder, but now I am not sure."

"I think my parable was badly phrased, Antiphon, and already I repent of it. For if you remember, I suggested as an 'inspiration' or 'incentive' to the man that he should think of the finished product, or arrange to have himself put to shame by his friends or nagged by his wife or commanded by the gods. And I implied, at least, that these were not reasons but just incentives. But now it appears, does it not, that they are reasons after all. Only, they are reasons of a different kind—not specifically connected with bridge-building, we might say, but reasons that might be used for doing any piece of work, just as you might have reasons for doing anything your father told you to."

"That is not much clearer, Socrates. But now I am anxious to pursue the 'good reasons in themselves,' as you call them, if my father is willing."

"How do you say, Cephalus?"

"Certainly, Socrates, but I must confess that I cannot for

the life of me see what they can be. I mean, I am clear about going to bed and putting down knives and trivial things of this kind, but what reason could there be for pursuing one whole way of life rather than another? Most of us, I suppose, have just accepted our morality from our fathers—or else we rebel against it, like Antiphon here, and when one ceases to accept it in this way, it must surely leave an uncomfortable gap in the soul. I at least feel very uncertain and empty about it."

"That is a very important point, Cephalus; so important, indeed, that I think we must give it a full consideration tomorrow. For now it is time for bed—though I do not think you need issue any stern commands to Antiphon here, who has already proved himself a full-grown and sensible person. Indeed, Cephalus, you are much to be commended for producing and educating such a son."

"Good-night, then, Socrates."

*   *   *

When we met the next day, I began by saying: "Well, Cephalus and Antiphon, do you still wish to continue our conversation?"

"Good heavens, yes," said Antiphon. "How could you think otherwise, Socrates?"

"Well, I wondered if perhaps you were becoming a little alarmed. For, after all, we have not yet discovered the basis of morality and life—and yet we still have to go on living. I wondered if you were perhaps feeling like those sailors of Carthage that Herodotus speaks of."

"Which are those?"

How to Use the Map

"The ones who set out to sail around Africa. They had a map, you see, made by Hecataeus or someone else, but as they progressed on their voyage it seemed to them that the map did not represent what was really there at all, but was—partly, at least—just an invention."

"That often happens with maps."

"Yes, indeed. Well, some of the sailors—particularly the older ones, who had been taught to trust the map-makers—wanted to go on using the map, swearing that it was all true even if it seemed otherwise. Others of them, the younger and bolder sort, were for throwing the map overboard and using their own judgment. But the captain disagreed with both."

"What did the captain say?"

"He saw that the map was inaccurate, at least in places, but he saw no reason for getting rid of it altogether. He said to the older men—as it might be you, Cephalus—'Friends, I know you have been brought up to believe in maps such as these, but it does appear at least possible, does it not, that we cannot take it entirely on trust. At least we must examine it and judge for ourselves.' And to the younger—like you, Antiphon—he said: 'I agree with you younger men that we must use our own judgment, but surely that does not mean that we must throw the map overboard. Let us, indeed, no longer treat it as something infallible, but let us from time to time examine it, for it may still be of help to us.' That is what the captain said."

"Well, Cephalus, it seems that Socrates is putting us to school again. This story of his refers, I take it, to what you were saying yesterday, toward the end of our talk. If you remember, you were saying how empty it made one feel not to have a very simple and comforting creed which one could always rely on—like the map in the story."

"Yes, Antiphon, but the younger men were foolish, were they not?"

"It seems so, but which of the two is better, Socrates?"

Young People Equally "Authoritarian"

"Antiphon, I think you have missed the point of my little tale. I was trying to suggest that it was, in reality, equally alarming for both. Look here, Antiphon, do you think that young people are less religious than their elders, and less inclined to rely on authority?"

"I do, yes."

"So that they do not have this feeling of emptiness and alarm of which Cephalus spoke—as if they had no solid food or substance within themselves? For that is what it is like, is it not? Well, then, do young men have none of this feeling, but charge boldly ahead on their own, thinking and reasoning fearlessly like free and strong men?"

"Perhaps not as much as I thought, Socrates."

"Perhaps not. But let us consider. Do the young men dress in a way which they think is most pleasing to the eye of other people, or do they dress according to some other principle?"

"Such as what?"

"Well, I have heard that many of them wear a kind of uniform, as it were, with certain kinds of boots and trousers and hair-styles, each looking much like his fellows, so as to be recognizable as a member of a certain group. Others again seem to follow the principle of dressing in a way exactly contrary to their parents. They take great time and trouble in making themselves look untidy, and are careful to put holes in their tunics and never to wear anything which might make them look like businessmen. The young women, too, I have heard, follow the fashions very diligently."

"Quite true, Socrates."

"And do they not also follow fashions in music and other such things? I mean, is it important to them to have heard the latest compositions and to be well up in whatever trend is current?"

"It is, very."

"And do they not also entertain various beliefs, such as a belief in astrology, or in the words of Marx, or in the 'liberation' (as they call it) of various groups of people? So that one might be excused for calling them just as religious as their elders, only in a different style."

"I suppose so."

"And might this not be because they too share this empty feeling we talked of? They are united, like the younger sailors and the map, in throwing away the authority which used to be acceptable. But it seems to me that they have accepted new authorities of their own—the opinion of their age-group, perhaps, or various ideas and fantasies which bubble up from their souls, as from hot and seething springs?"

"That looks very plausible, Socrates."

"Well, what are we to do? Shall we say something like this to them: 'Young men'—and we must add young women, since it is often difficult to tell them apart these days— 'we are engaged in a search for the basis of morality. We have reason to doubt, as you do, the old authorities and beliefs, but also, we are not very anxious to set up new authorities too quickly, until we have examined them thoroughly. So if you are willing to join with us in our search, we welcome you. But I am afraid the search will be a long one, so that we must ask you to lay aside your new gods for the time being in order that we can pay attention to the problems that lie before us.' Shall we say that?"

"Yes, but you will have a hard job to make them listen."

"Just as you younger men find it hard to persuade your fathers to listen, Antiphon. But perhaps, in both cases, it is because they did not start young enough. If they had been induced to join our search to the best of their ability when they were younger, maybe they would not cling so tightly to their gods and idols."

"Well, but how do you persuade them to join in the search?"

"Hold on, Antiphon! We have not progressed far in it ourselves yet, so that we shall not be able to lead the way. Surely we must first search further ourselves and then, when we have found the truth, we can communicate it to the young."

Here Cephalus broke in with great eagerness:

Discussion or Argument Itself Involves Morality

"Hey, Socrates! I think I have something important to say. You are wrong, you know, in what you just said."

"Well, that is always important—to me, at any rate. But in what way did I go wrong?"

"You implied that we had no idea of the basis of morality and would have to find it for ourselves before we had anything to offer to the young."

"And isn't that correct?"

"No, by the gods! For might it not be—or am I being too daring?—that the actual process of searching itself is part of that basis?"

"Steady on, Cephalus; you're going too fast for me."

"I mean this: Are we not now discussing and searching, all three of us, in our conversation? And does this not require from us a certain kind of behavior—even a morality—without which we could not converse? For instance, when Antiphon and I were quarreling the other day, the argument could not proceed. And if we were to try to kill each other, or were drunk all the time, or took no account of what each other had said, then we could not search properly, could we?"

"No, we could not."

"Then are there not some things at least which reason requires us all to do, Socrates—not to kill each other, and so on—without which we cannot even ask and answer questions sensibly? I would perhaps put this myself by talking of the laws that Zeus has laid down for conversation and entertainment, and what certain 'good sages' have said about treating your neighbor as an equal, but put it how you like."

"A very interesting idea, Cephalus. But what if a man does not want to search for the truth, as we are doing?"

"Well, Socrates, of course there are many such people. But you could not call them reasonable or sensible, could you? I mean, truth must surely be valuable to any man—just like Antiphon's strength and freedom that we were talking about. So that if a man is not interested in truth, he cannot have any good reasons for his morality—indeed he is not concerned with reasons at all."

"You seem right in what you say. So then, we seem justified in transmitting this at least to young people—that is, whatever is required for us to communicate and discuss effectively. And, now that I think of it, there are many abilities and aptitudes involved in such discussion, so that we shall have our hands full enough."

"But that can't be all, Socrates, though I stand by what I have just said."

"How do you mean?"

But What "Good Reasons" Are Peculiar to Morals?

"Well, let us suppose that we were trying to teach the young science or mathematics or any other of the arts and sciences. Then certainly we should have to begin by ensuring that they listened to their teachers, and that they could ask and answer questions sensibly with them, and in general discuss them in the sort of way that we have just been saying. But we would do more also; that would only be a sort of foundation for the subject. We should want to go on to teach them (if we knew) how to think rightly about the particular subject—science or mathematics or whatever it was—and what principles to follow in it."

"Yes, we should."

"So that at this stage we would need to be clearer about the 'good reasons in themselves' that you mentioned in the case of morality, Socrates. Otherwise, we can imagine the young saying something like this: 'O Cephalus and Socrates and Antiphon, you have taught us to think and discuss things generally; we are not fighting or quarreling, and indeed it is a pleasure for us to talk with such nice people as yourselves. Moreover, we quite see that we need to search for the truth about the basis of morality, as you have been doing. But can't you help us a little further? Our teachers of science and mathematics and other subjects have shown us very clearly how to pursue our studies there. We know well enough how to do those subjects and what counts as a good reason in each one of them. Now, does none of you know enough to tell us what counts as a good reason in morality—that is, what the basis of the subject is? Or are you here as pupils, and we are supposed to teach you?' And what should we say to them then, Socrates?"

"Well, Cephalus, I think we might have something to say to them, but I should like more time to consider just what. It has been a long day, and we have covered a lot of ground."

CHAPTER 3

Moral Reasoning and Divine Law

"Hello again, Socrates." Antiphon and I have been particularly looking forward to your visit today, since we are to discuss the nature of good reasons in morality, are we not?"

"I think I may have to disappoint you, Cephalus, for there is one matter which seems to come before that subject, which we have not considered at all."

"And what is that?"

What Is Morality?

"Well, what exactly is this 'morality' whose basis we are trying to find? What do we mean by the word?"

"Surely what is not a very difficult question, Socrates. Everybody knows what it means to call something 'moral' or 'immoral'; these are common words, like 'good' and 'bad' and 'right' and 'wrong.'"

"Tell me, Cephalus, do you know what air is made of?"

"Air? No, I don't know. I don't think anyone does."

"What about the chryselephantine statue of Athene, which Pheidias made and placed in the Parthenon?"

"That is easy, Socrates. As the word implies, it is made of gold and ivory, no doubt with the addition of some other things, such as paint and so on."

"And yet air is very common, whereas the statue of Athene is uncommon—indeed, it is unique. So perhaps we may be ignorant about common things, even if they are very close to us—just as a man may search everywhere for his hat, not knowing that he has already put it on his head."

"Very well, Socrates, you know best; ask away."

"I do not at all know best, Cephalus, but I will ask. And if matters are as easy as you maintain, you will no doubt be able to clear things up for me in no time at all. Well, now, what do you mean by this common word 'moral'?"

"I mean, like everyone else, what is in accordance with the customs and values of our society, Socrates. For instance, it is moral to have one wife, and cover up one's body in the right places, and to repay debts. And it is immoral to steal, and to allow one's wife to walk around the streets by herself, and so on."

Here Antiphon interrupted:

Not Just Accepting a Particular Tradition

"We shall certainly have a quick end to the argument, Socrates, if we are to follow Cephalus here; at least so far as I am concerned."

"Why is that, Antiphon?"

"Because if he means by 'moral' and 'morality' those

customs and traditions which operate in our society, then I am not interested in finding a basis for morality in that sense. For I do not approve of the customs, or at least not all of them."

"It seems that we shall have to give some other answer then, Cephalus. For do we not wish to discuss with Antiphon, among other things, whether such customs are right or wrong?"

"I suppose so, Socrates. And yet I thought my account of the words 'moral' and 'immoral' was not too wide of the mark. Surely, whatever Antiphon thinks, it is ridiculous to say that it is 'moral' to go around naked, or 'immoral' to keep slaves or repay one's debts."

"I think you are right, Cephalus. But perhaps the word has more than one meaning. Tell me, science is not the same as painting, is it?"

"Of course not."

"Painting is an art, not a science."

"I suppose so, though to judge by some modern painters, it is not even that. Do you know, Socrates, there is one painter who does not use brushes at all; he just pours out all his paint onto a large sheet of cardboard, and then drags naked women over it?"

"Perhaps he is very poor, Cephalus, and cannot afford brushes; or perhaps he is modestly trying to cover up the women in some way, not being able to afford clothes for them. But we are straying from the point. I was saying that painting was not scientific, as astronomy and other things are."

"Correct."

"Is it then unscientific? Would you use that word about it?"

"I suppose so."

"But it might mislead, might it not? For we blame people for being unscientific when they are doing things that belong to science but doing them badly. But we would not want to blame Zeuxis or some other painter in these terms."

"No."

"Would it not be more precise to call painting nonscientific? For that has no element of blame about it."

"If you like."

"And in the same way we would not blame animals for being unreasonable or irrational, would we, since they do not partake of reason at all. We should be more precise in saying that they were nonrational, or nonreasonable."

"Yes, I see."

But a General Area of Human Thought and Action

"Well, then, is there not a sense of 'moral' which is like 'scientific'? I mean, which describes, not the performance of a citizen who obeys the laws and customs of our society, but something else?"

"What else?"

"Some general area of thought and behavior, Cephalus; perhaps it is one of the arts and sciences, or perhaps it is something else. For instance, how one plays draughts is not a matter of morality, is it?"

"No, unless you cheat."

"Yet would you describe a bad draughts-player as immoral?"

"No."

"If one wanted to describe him in terms of morality at all, would we not have to use some term like 'nonmoral,' thereby showing that we did not think that draughts entered into the moral area?"

"Yes."

"Very well, then. We now have another sense for 'morality' and 'moral,' not to do with the customs and traditions of our society, but with something else."

"What else, Socrates? I am puzzled."

"Well, Cephalus, that is a hard question. We can, I suppose, define the area of human life which we are going to call 'moral' in many different ways. I have heard, indeed, that there are some societies among the barbarians who think that the kind of food one eats is a moral matter. The sophists in our city have argued at great length about the word, some claiming that it has to do with public reproach and blame, others that it has to do with what holds society together, and so on. But I propose to cut short the dispute."

"In what way?"

"I think we can escape from it like the Scythian slave if only we keep our eye on our main objective."

"Which slave was this?"

"A runaway from Athens, Cephalus, who escaped across the border to Thebes. He was pursued by two policemen, who must have been trained by the sophists. For they came to an inn on the border which had a sign reading, 'Runaway slaves welcome here.' One policeman thought that the slave had gone into the inn, and wanted to search it, but the other said, 'No, that is what he wants us to think. These slaves are cunning; he hopes that we shall waste time here while he escapes.' 'No,' said the first, 'the slave may be very cunning—he will expect you to argue like that and has actually gone inside.' And so they disputed for some time. Meanwhile the slave, who could not read and hence had

least we know what sort of reasons are to count as good reasons in morality, if only in the most general way—that is, those reasons which relate to human interests and needs and not to something else. For instance, if we asked a man whether we ought to fight the Persians, and he replied that we ought, and when we asked him why, he said something like, 'Because seven sevens are forty-nine,' what would we say?"

"That he was mad, I suppose."

"Probably, Antiphon, and yet there are many people who border on such madness. Have you never met people who think it is very important not to have odd numbers to their houses, or who have what they call 'lucky numbers'? And think of the saying 'third time lucky,' and all that the Pythagoreans say about the merits of certain numbers and the evil done by others. But anyway, suppose we are kind to him; would we not say 'O man, what you say about seven sevens is most interesting and well worth knowing, but just now we are not interested in mathematics—we want to know what is the best thing for us and the Persians and surely these numbers have nothing to do with it.' Could we not fairly say that?"

"I think we could, and more besides."

"Well, then, we have cleared one hurdle in our obstacle race. But another is to come, which we must leave till later."

*   *   *

"Well, Socrates, Antiphon and I have been discussing what we said yesterday, and we came to the conclusion that you had said nothing very spectacular."

"How kind of you, Cephalus."

"Kind? I was making a criticism. Certainly we agree that

morality is to do with human wants and interests and the like. That is obvious enough, but surely it is hardly worth saying."

"Can you see air, Cephalus?"

"Why do you keep asking me about air, Socrates? What has that got to do with it?"

"Please do not get upset, Cephalus, but just answer."

"No, of course not."

"So it is not very spectacular, is it? And I suppose the same might be said of many ordinary things, like blood and bread and water and many others. Yet without these we should die, should we not? The chryselephantine statue of Pheidias is certainly spectacular, but not more important than these humble things."

"Well, Socrates, I am schooled. But can we not advance the argument further?"

Mysticism No Substitute for Philosophy

"I hope so, indeed. But I would not want you to think that I have been harsh with you. Why, I myself only recently was very taken with what was spectacular in philosophy. I used to read the works of the mystics and other magniloquent writers who painted the most beautiful word-pictures which went straight to my heart, so that I felt really inspired. I used to listen for hours to the declamations which they made in temples and other beautiful places—often accompanied by glorious music and other lovely things. But later I did not go quite as often as before."

"Why not?"

"That was just what one of my older friends asked me. I replied to him, as to you now, that I did indeed feel the need, on occasion, for elevated words and music of this kind, for it is a hard, work-a-day world we live in, with much evil in it, so that our souls can be refreshed by such means and we can be exalted, if only for a time. But (I said) it seemed to me that these mystics and others were not much concerned with what was true. They gave no reasons or arguments, but were content merely to paint these beautiful, other-worldly pictures with their words and sounds. And I found that I did better to go into the market-place and argue there to find the truth, or to the houses of my friends. Mysticism has its place, and a very important place too, to nourish our imagination and keep us from despair. But truth is something else, which has to be worked for."

"Then work away."

Human Wants Ought To Be Satisfied

"I hope you will join me in the task. Now, each of us wants to be happy and have his wants and interests satisfied, does he not?"

"Of course."

"But does he have any reasons for satisfying his wants, or is he driven to do so blindly, like a beast?"

"What an odd question, Socrates!"

"It is odd, I agree, but perhaps worth asking, just the same. I mean, does he think it right that his wants should be satisfied, or that he ought to satisfy them? Or does he just charge ahead and satisfy them?"

"Well, I suppose that—if he thinks at all—he must think that it is right to satisfy them."

"All men have wants, do they not?"

"They do."

"Now tell me, if I walk off a cliff I will fall downwards, will I not?"

"Yes, Socrates, through the air! Really, what with air and cliffs, I will lose the thread of the argument."

"Will I fall downward only because it is I, Socrates, who is there?"

"No, that is not the reason."

"Then what is?"

"All men have weight, and anything with weight falls downwards through the air."

"So it is not that I am Socrates, but the fact that I have weight which makes it reasonable to believe that I shall fall downwards?"

"Yes, of course."

"Let us set this out more precisely, if you don't mind, Cephalus. It is a chain of reasoning like this, isn't it: All things that have weight fall; I have weight; therefore I shall fall. Is that right?"

"Yes."

And Not Just One's Own Wants, but Wants in General

"Now let us apply this to the satisfaction of wants. If I think I ought to satisfy my wants, can that be only because they are mine?"

"Well, Socrates, it is a very common thing for people to satisfy their own wants and not to bother about anyone else's."

"I do not deny that, Cephalus, but I did not ask whether people did satisfy their wants, but whether they thought that they ought to do so, and, if they did, why."

"Very well, Socrates; I suppose you want me to say that I ought to satisfy my wants, not because they are mine, but because wants in general ought to be satisfied, and I am only one case of this."

"I do not want you to say anything you do not mean, Cephalus. But we are talking, aren't we, about what it is to have a reason—that was why I used the example of falling off a cliff. I was suggesting that any reason must have a general nature, as it were. I cannot use such things as, 'Because my name is Socrates,' or 'Because it is noon,' or 'Because I am standing here' as reasons unless I can give them some general force."

"How do you mean, a general force?"

"Well, if everybody whose name began with S was being called up to fight the Persians, then it might be a reason to say, 'My name is Socrates.' The chain would be: All those with names beginning with S must go to war; my name is Socrates, which begins with an S; therefore I must go to war. But my point is, there must be some such chain."

"What is the chain that applies to human wants and needs, then?"

"I think it is something like this: Wants and needs and interests (I am not quite sure which, Cephalus) in general ought to be satisfied; I have some wants and needs and interests; therefore my wants and needs and interests ought to be satisfied. That is, the reason for my satisfying them is not that they are mine, but that they are just one case—the nearest one, from my point of view—of wants and so on in general."

"Yes."

"But does Antiphon agree?"

"Yes, Socrates, and I think I can take the argument further. You will not like it, though."

"Then I shall have to learn to put up with it, if it is true. For our likes and dislikes are neither here nor there."

"Well, it seems to follow, Socrates, that all men's wants and interests and so on—let us say 'wants' for short—are of equal importance. For the major premise of the chain you mentioned just now was precisely that, wasn't it?"

"Explain more fully, if you please."

"Well, to use your own example, have I any more reason to believe that I will fall off the cliff (if I walk over it) than that you will, or vice versa?"

"No, for both of us have weight."

"Just so, and even though our weight may not be equal, that makes no matter; it is having weight—any weight—that counts."

"Yes."

"So, if we say that wants in general must be satisfied—that is the only reason I have for satisfying my own wants—then other people's wants are just as important as my own?"

"It seems so."

"But are you not alarmed, Socrates? For—to take just one example—what about the wants of all those slaves which we possess? Do you think they want to be slaves, or that it makes them happy? Of course not. It is we who tyrannize over them, considering our own wants and interests and not theirs at all."

"Good gracious, Antiphon, I believe you may be right."

"I am not so simple-minded, Socrates, as to suppose that this is news to you. I believe that you have held this view all along and just wanted someone else to produce it for you, in your usual way."

A Possible Difficulty

"Well, but might not one object to this? I think if I were to ask Nicias, who is extremely clever and possesses a great many slaves (indeed, he would not be rich at all otherwise), he might say something like this: 'O Socrates and Antiphon, I quite see the force of your arguments. I see that I must have a chain of reasoning, as you call it. But, gentlemen, the first link in my chain is not quite the same as what you suggest. It is not, 'All people's wants should be satisfied,' but rather, 'The wants of all free citizens should be satisfied. Slaves, in my view, do not count.' What could we say to him?"

"Heavens, Socrates, I don't know. And I thought I had everything quite settled!"

"Cephalus, can you come to your son's aid in this affair?"

"I will try, Socrates. I think it is like that earlier occasion, when the same argument reappears at another level. There are two things one might say to Nicias; one of them I feel fairly certain of, but about the other I am not sure."

"Let us have the certain one first, then."

Answered by Cephalus

"Well, I should say this: 'O Nicias, you are a clever man and naturally entitled to your views. But do you think that your slaves are entitled to theirs? For they would be likely to disagree with you on this matter.' "

"He would say, wouldn't he, that slaves were not entitled to have any views, or, at least, that no weight should be attached to them."

"Then I should add this, Socrates: 'You have misunderstood me, Nicias. It was this very view I was asking about—that is, your view that slaves were not entitled to have views. Do you have any reason for considering yourself entitled to hold that opinion? And now you cannot say it is because you are a free man, for it is just that which I am asking you about.' Would he not have to say, Socrates, that he did feel entitled—and now, not because he was a free man, but just because he was a man? Certainly, if he was honest that is what he would say. For all men think that their views ought to count and be attended to."

"Very good, Cephalus! But what about your second argument, the less certain one?"

"Perhaps it is really the same as the first, Socrates. But it seems to me that holding a view, or having a major premise in the chain of reasoning, is not unlike having a want; it is surely something the person desires to use in his thought and life. Now, does he have any reason for *this* want? Nicias wants to use his premise, and the slaves a different one. Of course they may argue together, and one may persuade the other that he is the wiser, but if this does not happen— when both sides have run out of reasons, so to speak— must they not compromise? Just as, when both armies have run out of ammunition, it is best to patch up a peace. For now, what conceivable reason could each have for satisfying his own wants, other than that he is simply a human being? But this implies, as we said, that all human wants are important."

"What a father you have, Antiphon! Did you know he could talk like this?"

"No, I did not, Socrates, but whether he is right or wrong, that is the sort of talk I like to hear rather than the quarrels we used to have. But is he right?"

"I believe he is, Antiphon. It will need working out much more carefully at another time, but for the present perhaps we may take it that—so far as reason goes—all human beings are equal. I do not mean, of course, that they are all equally wise or rich or heavy or anything like that, but rather that they count equally with each other in respect of their needs and wants. Whether or not the modern democrats have that in mind when they talk of equality, I do not know, but it seems important, anyway."

"There is one thing that puzzles me, Socrates. If all this is so, how is it that people do not behave in this way? We should expect to see them behaving kindly to each other, knowing that the other's wants are as important as their own, but in fact we see them trying to get as much as they can for themselves. And another thing is just as puzzling; even though they behave in this selfish manner, they all pay lip-service to what we have just said—I do not mean the reasons for it, but just the conclusion, that all human beings should count."

Why the Principle Is Neglected in Practice

"I think I can enlighten you, Antiphon. It is surely that, although the truth of what we are saying is perhaps obvious enough (even without Cephalus' subtle arguments), people find it very hard to keep it steadily in their minds. Most people, you know, do not really think at all. What is most real to them is their own wants and desires. These are pressing and urgent, and other people are far less real. When they feel hungry, they grab food for themselves. Certainly, if they took time to reflect they might say to themselves, 'My own hunger is only a reason for my taking food, because hunger in general is a reason, and look, here are other hungry people! We must divide the food equally.' But in practice they do not reflect. Perhaps a large part of what we have to teach the young is simply to reflect in general. Then they may acquire the habit and will reflect about morality in particular."

"But what about the other point?"

"You mean, the lip-service they pay to the equality of human needs? Well, Antiphon, perhaps this is a lesson they have learned from the rulers or the priests or other people of that kind. It may be that the rulers have found it too difficult to teach people the real reasons for what we have established—though, frankly, they seem simple enough, and it may be just that they have not really tried. So, as parents often do, they have made use of mercenary reasons."

"How do you mean, mercenary?"

"I mean, reasons which will produce the required action, even though by the operation of some outside force—just as mercenary soldiers will win wars when the citizens are too lazy or weak to fight themselves. Perhaps the rulers and the priests have told the people that the gods wish them to be kind to one another and treat each other as equals (though not the rulers). Or perhaps they have educated them to feel ashamed and guilty if they are too openly selfish. So that, in their words if not in their deeds, most people will be found to accept that other men's wants should count, or that men should be treated as brothers. If you ask them why, they do not really know, though many will talk of faith, or intuition, or something of that kind."

"It is probably more complicated than that, Socrates. But anyway, Cephalus and I must go out to look after our farms now. We will resume tomorrow."

* * *

"Well, Antiphon, and how are your farms?"

"Not too bad, Socrates. But since I have become more interested in them, I have begun to see just how difficult farming is—if you are going to do it properly, I mean. Hitherto, I am ashamed to say, I regarded my father's farms as merely a gentleman's plaything—rather like a young child who thinks that shields and spears and chariots and the like are just toys, put there for his own benefit and amusement. But now that I know what farming is about, I see what a lot I have to learn."

"How wise your son is, Cephalus! And yet how simple-minded also."

"What can you mean, Socrates?"

"Well, if someone had come to him a few years ago, asking, 'Antiphon, can you tell me the difference between the art of farming and the art of amusing oneself or playing with toys?' he would have known well enough what to reply, would he not?"

"I imagine so."

"He would have said, 'Certainly my friend. Farming is about how to produce good crops and cattle and that sort of thing; amusing oneself is something quite different.' So he knew well enough even then. But for some reason or other that simple knowledge was not enough for him. Whereas now he has become wise, as well as simple-minded; he keeps this knowledge firmly in his mind and is trying to build upon it."

"I see what you mean."

"And does this not give some hope to all of us, in regard to the art of living or morality? For with this art, at least, all men have to do."

"How so?"

"I mean that we need to cling to this simple knowledge. So that if someone were to ask us, saying 'O men of Athens, please tell us about the art of living. Has it to do with making a great deal of money, or acquiring honor and high positions, or perhaps with exercising power over other men? Or is it a matter of being respected by one's neighbors, or being as handsome as possible, or what?' If someone were to ask that, we should know what to say, should we not?"

"What should we say, then?"

Human Interests the Basis of Morality

"I had hoped that you would tell, Cephalus. It is true that we have not advanced very far in the argument, but I think perhaps we could at least say something like this: 'O man, it is a difficult question you asked us, but, so far as we can see, the art of living is not about any of the things you mention—or at least not directly. It has to do with the satisfaction of human needs and interests; not only one's own interests, but those of other people also. Now, it may be that money and honor and power and all the other things you mention help to satisfy human beings, but it is by no means certain, so that we shall have to examine each of them carefully and not take any for granted.'"

"Very true, Socrates. For I have found as I have grown older, that these things are like women who appear beautiful when seen from far off, but who on closer acquaintance turn out to be plain and boring. Certainly, a little money and enough food, and health, are important to men but thereafter I think that there are two things which I should regard as most important for the satisfaction you speak of."

"Which are they?"

"First, Socrates, to have work or some other activity which you enjoy, and second, to have people around you whom you love, and who love you. And of these I think the latter counts for more in the long run."

"Well, Antiphon, and what do you think?"

"I think Socrates, that my father may well be right. But each man must prove this for himself, must he not?"

"How do you mean?"

Some Human "Goods" Described

"Well, Socrates, I do not think that I can explain briefly. May I speak at greater length, or will you and Cephalus be bored?"

"How could we be bored in the pursuit of knowledge about how to live?"

"Very easily, most people are. Though whether they are really bored, or rather despair because the whole enterprise seems too difficult, I do not know. But anyway it seems to me that there are three things that might serve as a basis for the temple of morality, all of them being derived from this business of satisfying wants.

"First, Socrates, there are the things which a wise man of experience, like my father here, might come to see are truly important for man—such as love and work, for instance, rather than honor or power or respectability. I suppose that it could be disputed which things exactly these are, but if we knew what they were with certainty they could serve as a basis of some kind.

"Second, there are things which, on reflection, anybody can see to be absolutely necessary for the satisfaction of any wants whatever. I mean things like strength and freedom, which we mentioned before. And one might add other obvious things, such as security from danger, and various powers of body and mind which are useful for getting what one wants and helping other people as well."

Here Antiphon stopped and looked worried so that I said:

"Well, Antiphon, why do you stop at the last lap of the race? I thought you were going splendidly. I hope you are not going to do what that pair of Corinthian horses did to me the other day. I thought that I would win the bet I had placed on them, and indeed they were far ahead of the rest until near the end, but at that point—would you believe it?—they slowed to a walk and began to whinny and neigh to each other, for all the world as if they had human speech, like the horses of Achilles, and were more interested in discussion than in racing. The charioteer whipped them, but they would go no further. But you, my dear fellow, please tell us if you are in difficulties; we shall not whip you, I promise."

"Yes, Socrates, I am in trouble. For I thought I had everything nicely organized in three groups, but now I see that this is not so at all."

"What was your third group to be?"

"It was to consist of various mental abilities and competencies that were important for any man, and ought to be acquired—and, I thought, taught to young people."

"But did you not mention these briefly under your second heading, Antiphon, when you spoke of 'various powers of body and mind'?"

"Yes Socrates, and yet I still feel that they are different somehow."

"Perhaps I can help you. In your second category you wanted to place certain advantages or necessities, did you not—I mean, things which any man must have if he is to be happy—such as strength, and freedom, and security, and such things as health and indeed life itself, I suppose?"

"Yes."

"Tell me, Antiphon, one cannot seek for what is already found, can one?"

"Of course not."

"If one has it, one does not need to seek it?"

"No."

"And yet, I suppose, in life and morality nobody has everything that is good; we have not made life ideal either for ourselves or—what is also our duty, as we have seen—for other people. Indeed, this is very far from being the case, and I do not see how it ever could be. So it seems to follow that we must all spend a great deal of time in the seeking, as well as in the enjoyment of our goods and advantages. Perhaps this is particularly true of young people, who must inevitably spend much time and trouble in seeking and deciding what they ought to do."

"Yes."

The "Goods" Relevant to Wise Moral Choice

"Well, then, will there not be certain things which are required for just this enterprise—I mean the seeking and deciding what to do? And will not this give you a separate category? For instance, strength and security and health are certainly advantages, but they are not particularly concerned with seeking for answers and deciding things, are they?"

"In a way they are, Socrates. It is hard to decide anything sensibly if you are weak or ill."

"True, Antiphon, you do right to correct me. Well, shall we say that there are certain necessities—preconditions, let us call them—which must be satisfied if a man is to have the chance of thinking seriously and correctly, but that thinking and deciding also have special virtues of their own?"

"Very well."

"So, then, these special virtues—what a man requires in order to decide correctly what to do and then to act upon it—can perhaps form your third category. But will not this category be extremely important? In a way it seems to me it outshines all the rest."

"How so?"

"Tell me, which is more important: that your farm should have good crops, or that you should know how to grow good crops on your farm?"

"What a funny question! Both of them go together, surely."

"Not necessarily, Antiphon. For it may be that, through no fault of yours, the crops are ravaged by the Spartans, or perhaps you have to sell your land to the money-lenders, or something of that kind. But answer me this: Which would you rather bequeath to your son, when you have one—money, or the ability to make money?"

"The latter. For if I left him money only, he might run through it quickly and be poor afterwards, whereas if he had the ability to make money he could always do it for himself at any time."

These Are What the Young Need

"Well, is it not just the same with morality and the good life? If we can bequeath our young people the powers and abilities and competencies you spoke of—that is, those that are required for a man to make up his mind correctly and act on sensible decisions—might that not be better than simply bequeathing them the other goods? Though of course we should hope to do both."

"I think you are right, Socrates. And in this way we should not be imposing anything on the young, who will not take kindly to such imposition—and quite right, too. We should simply be giving them the power to make up their own minds more reasonably for themselves."

"Good, Antiphon. I agree with you. It seems, though, that now you have come to believe in the rules and principles of reason. I do not mean just what our own society or any other regards as reasonable, but what really is reasonable for any many anywhere. For the powers and abilities in your third category are required by reason, are they not?"

"Certainly."

"I hope, Antiphon, and you too Cephalus, that you will not be cross with me if I seem to go backwards in the argument at this point. For I am wondering what you would now say about the 'divine law,' as Cephalus called it. Well, Antiphon?"

"I still think that there is no such thing, Socrates."

"And you, Cephalus?"

"Well, Socrates, I would still like to believe in it as a basis for morality, but I confess that I am not so certain as I was."

"Oh, dear! I had hoped that you would both say the opposite. But still, if you think that we must try to pursue the matter this afternoon, for it needs special treatment."

"Very well, but I do not think you will change our minds."

* * *

When we reassembled, I was rather alarmed in case

Antiphon and Cephalus should still feel very strongly about the divine law and other such matters, for in my experience questions of religious belief always generate very violent passions. So I began by addressing Antiphon as follows:

"Tell me, what is your name?"

At this Antiphon looked amazed, and said:

"Sit down here in the shade, Socrates, where it is cool, and I will bring you some water. I am Antiphon, a friend of yours and this is my father, Cephalus. You will remember everything soon. Meanwhile, please do not try to talk, but just lie there and rest."

The Importance of Descriptions

"Well, then, Antiphon—or may I call you 'son of Cephalus?'"

"Whichever you like."

"Or could I use some other description, such as 'heir to the estates near Marathon,' or 'the boy who won the foot-race at the Isthmian games last year,' or 'a young friend of Socrates with fair hair, who. . . .'"

"Please, Socrates, do not try to talk any more. Father, will you not fetch a doctor?"

"I think, my boy, that Socrates is just pretending again and is not ill at all. Come on, Socrates, we are not children, you know."

"I never thought so, Cephalus, father of Antiphon, owner of the estates near Marathon. . . ."

"Yes, yes, Socrates, I am all these things, but what are you trying to say?"

"Oh, you do not mind whether I use one title or another? You do not insist on just the one?"

"Of course not. They are just different words for the same thing."

"But would you accept any description? What about 'that old curmudgeon who bullies his son,' for instance?"

"Well, I would hardly like that."

"I wonder now, whether this may not be relevant to that 'divine law' we were talking about, Cephalus. It might be in the one case, or in the other."

"What do you mean?"

The "Divine Law" Again

"Well, perhaps all that you want to say about the gods and obedience and the divine law and conscience and so on—let us just say 'divine law' for short—is simply another description of something which we would all accept, even Antiphon here. Or perhaps it is a bad description, like 'that old curmudgeon,' and so to be rejected. What do you think, Antiphon?"

"I think it is a bad description, or not a description at all of anything real, but a myth or story merely."

"Let us see, then. You think, do you not, Antiphon, that there are certain rules and principles to be followed in morality—for instance, the principle that other people's interests should count? And perhaps there are other principles also, which we have not yet discussed."

"Certainly I do."

"And are these principles important?"

"Of course."

These "Goods" or Principles Exist Independently of Men

"They are not just human principles, are they? I mean, they are not exactly the invention of one man or a group of men, as a man might build a pyramid or invent the water-clock? Are they not more like discoveries—something that already exists, which the rational man perceives to be true?"

"I suppose so."

"And are these principles to be obeyed?"

"Certainly they are."

"They are, then, in a way like laws, are they not? I do not mean that they have been invented by a lawgiver, like Solon or another. I mean rather that they are principles that exist independently of our own wills and desires, and that ought to be obeyed. In that respect they are like laws."

"Yes, if you like."

"Tell me now, Antiphon, have you heard of such words as 'sacred,' 'holy,' 'to be revered,' and so on?"

"Yes, but I do not make much use of them, since they are usually applied to the gods, in whom I do not believe."

"Very good, but do you always make your slaves do the same tasks?"

"What? No, of course not."

"Of course, the way in which a slave works, and his strength and abilities, will be the same whatever he does— you cannot change those—but you can apply him to various tasks, can you not? I mean, you can use his powers to improve your house, or your crops, or many other things."

"Yes."

"It is just the same with words of this kind, Antiphon. You cannot change their force or their meaning. You cannot make 'sacred' mean 'stupid' or 'square,' for instance, but there is no reason why you should not apply the word to any person or thing that you wish. In one barbarian country, you know, they have an empty tomb or cenotaph, which contains absolutely nothing at all. Yet they hold it sacred, and conduct various rituals and ceremonies about it. These same barbarians also have colleges of wise men who follow many sacred rules concerning dress and food and passing the wine round to each other—from right to left, or perhaps left to right, I always forget which it is. Sometimes this seems to be a sort of game or joke, but sometimes not."

"Very well, Socrates, but what follows?"

And Might Be Called "Divine Law"

"Why, this, my dear fellow: If you think, as you seem to, that these rules and principles of morality are so important and valuable, why can we not say that they are 'to be revered,' or held 'sacred,' or counted as 'holy,' and so forth? Or do you think that other things are more important?"

"No, by Zeus; these are much the most important. They are worth more than all the foolish religious rituals and mumbo-jumbo which we have today."

"Then I advise you to use what weapons you have, Antiphon. You would not allow your neighboring farmers to have a monopoly on wheat or cattle or anything else, would you?"

"No."

"Then do you propose to hand over all these words—I mean 'holy' and the like—to the men of religion, so that they may hold the monopoly of them? Would it not be better for you to call sacred and holy that which you think of overwhelming importance—these rules and principles we are talking of—and let them call sacred and holy whatever they want to dignify by those titles?"

"Perhaps so."

"Then you could perhaps argue with them more easily,

saying, 'O men of religion, I do not at all want to deny that some things are sacred and to be revered. Indeed, if to believe this is to have a religion, then I must count myself as religious along with you. But I differ from you in regard to those things which ought to be called sacred. So come, let us discuss and argue together and see which of us is right.'"

"Yes, I could proceed in that way."

"It seems to me, Antiphon, that you are no longer a child frightened of shadows."

"What do you mean?"

"I mean that before you jerked away from words like 'divine law' like a child or a startled horse. But now you have admitted, first, that these principles are in some ways like laws, and second, that they are to be counted as sacred and holy and in some sense divine."

"I have not quite admitted the last of those words, Socrates, but never mind. Anyway, my father will be pleased now that his 'divine law' has been reinstated."

"Are you pleased, Cephalus?"

Morality Not Derived from Religion

"Very pleased indeed, Socrates. I always knew that morality had to have a religious basis."

"But I should not rejoice too quickly if I were you, for it may lead you to say what is not true."

"What?"

"You said 'a religious *basis*,' and I can't think you mean precisely that. We have shown, have we not, that the good life (or morality) depends—like everything else that men can know—on certain kinds of 'good reasons' for acting, concerned with human needs and interests. That is its logical basis, though as we saw we may also seek for mercenary reasons or incentives to keep us up to the mark."

"Yes, I had forgotten."

"What we have shown is, not that morality is based on religion, exactly, but perhaps that it is itself religious. I mean, that it is something very high and sacred and valuable, which stands above all men, in a sense, and is greatly to be admired and revered. I do not mind, as Antiphon does not, if we call this 'divine law,' or 'the most important principles of life,' or by any other name or description—provided it does not mislead us. I fear, though, that it may have misled many in the past."

"How, Socrates?"

But a Matter of Reason and Personal Decision

"Not sophisticated people like yourself and Antiphon, of course, but the simple and the weak, who like to be told what to do by other men. For, to be honest, Cephalus, isn't that how 'divine law' has been understood by many people? Have they not wanted to obey this 'law,' not because they thought it right, but just because it was there? It is like what we were saying earlier: Life is difficult and people want quick and certain answers, so that they are tempted to invent some very powerful and authoritative thing—perhaps a person, or perhaps some sort of natural force—who will do their thinking for them, and enforce certain answers on them."

"Perhaps so. But suppose there is such a person or thing?"

"Even if there were, Cephalus, it would make no difference, as we have seen. For we should still have to decide for ourselves whether to follow his laws or not. And how could we decide this properly, except by working out for ourselves what the true principles of morality were?"

"I suppose you are right. But it is easy to see why men usually shun this task. It is, as you say, very difficult. People feel weak and empty, and seek help from outside, and if they are not lucky enough to have friends who love them and aid them, they will perhaps hope for some supernatural or magical assistance. But do you think we can ever persuade them to do otherwise, Socrates?"

"Courage, my friend! Remember that in other departments of human life we have made some progress, and there is no reason why we should not do the same in morality. Why, it was not so long ago that there was no such thing as science. Instead of making observations and reflecting and obeying all the other principles that belong to science, men despaired of making sense of the physical world (or perhaps they were just lazy). For instance, instead of seriously trying to find out what makes the Nile flood, they kept themselves happy by saying such things as, 'The god Ra causes it,' or 'Our prayers have worked again.' So, too, with mathematics. The Egyptians did not know why a triangle with sides of 3, 4, and 5 cubits long should make a right angle; they called it 'the will of the gods' and said that it was a 'divine law.' And so, in a sense, it is, but now Pythagoras has shown us what the rule is. Any number will do, provided that the squares of two of them add up to the square of the third—that is the rule. So I have some hope that we can conduct the same operation with morality. Perhaps tomorrow we can pursue this further."

CHAPTER 4

Moral Aptitudes and Virtues

"Good morning, Socrates. I trust you slept well."

"Not very well, Cephalus, I am afraid. For I had a long dream which troubled me greatly."

"And what dream was that?"

The Virtues

"Well, it appeared to me that a large number of beautiful women or goddesses were standing round my bed, entreating me to listen to them."

"I cannot see why that should have troubled you, Socrates! Unless because there were too many of them, of course."

"No, but they seemed more interested in possessing my soul than my body, Cephalus. As for my body, I do not reckon much to that—anybody may have it who wants. But I cannot devote my soul or my mind to just anything. And this is what these women seemed to want."

"Who were they?"

"At first I did not know, but as my dream became clearer I saw that each had her name written in letters of gold on her forehead. They were, it appeared, those goddesses whom we call the Virtues. There were older, more respectable virtues, such as Temperance and Wisdom, and Courage and Justice and the like, and some newer ones with names I had not heard before, like Creativity and Self-Expression, and there were also some extremely bleak-looking ladies called Juvenile Decency and Hygenic Child-Rearing. But all of them addressed me with one voice, saying: 'You ought to be ashamed of yourself, Socrates! For you have been discussing morality all this time with Cephalus and your other friends and never a mention of us! Yet surely, if true morality lodges anywhere, it lodges with us; it is we whom mortal men need and not any of the other things you have talked about.'"

"And how did you reply to them?"

"Well, I was not sure at first, but after a little I plucked up courage and said: 'Ladies, you are all outstandingly beautiful, and I am sure that you are right to rebuke me for paying so little attention to you. The fact is, I am a nervous man and reluctant to offend any one of you. You remember how much trouble Paris caused when he had to choose between three goddesses, so naturally I am hesitant. For I am sure you will agree that it will sometimes be necessary to make a choice. Thus I might act as Temperance prompts, but Courage would perhaps disagree, and Creativity or Self-Expression might bid my children to do certain things which Juvenile Decency would not like at all. So, then, I am sure you will forgive me if I leave you for the time being. I will return later and pay you all due honor.' That is what I said."

There Are No Rules Without Exceptions

"Hmm, Socrates, I am not sure about that."

"About what, Cephalus?"

"Well, surely we know that some of these goddesses at least are to be revered? I mean, we know that truthfulness and justice and honesty are good things."

"Always, Cephalus, or only sometimes?"

"Always, surely."

"Answer me then, Cephalus; truthfulness does not involve lying, does it, nor does honesty involve stealing?"

"Of course not."

"Now suppose a criminal came in with a sword, and you and Antiphon were sitting there, and he said, 'I'm going to kill Antiphon; is this he?'—would you tell him the truth?"

"No."

"And suppose you were able to steal the Persian general's plans in wartime, so as to stop the war and save our city, would you not do that?"

"Yes."

"So, then, it seems as if these goddesses ought not always to be obeyed. Usually, perhaps, but not always. But how are the young to know when to obey and when to disobey? For the goddesses themselves will not teach them."

"It seems to me, Socrates, that we must give the young other guides which are more infallible, so that they can make up their own minds correctly."

"Right, Cephalus, and perhaps Antiphon can help us say what these other guides are. Antiphon, what guides do you think we have identified already in our argument?"

"There is only the one, Socrates, that is clear to me; namely, that what we decide to do should be governed by what is in the interests of ourselves and other people."

"Antiphon, do you grow all your crops in the same field?"

"Certainly not, Socrates. Why do you ask?"

"Because I think that this one phrase, 'the interests of ourselves and other people,' may yield many crops, of different kinds. Perhaps they need sorting out and putting in order."

"Go on, then."

The Concept of a Person

"Well, could somebody be concerned with other people if he did not know what a person was?"

"No, but surely everyone knows that."

"What is it, then?"

"A human being, like ourselves, with arms and legs. Stop fooling about, Socrates, and get on with the argument."

"No doubt I am foolish, Antiphon, but I am not trying to be, I assure you. Tell me, have you heard of Antibolus?"

"I know him very well; a fine man."

"Yet he lost almost all his limbs fighting the Persians, so either we must say that he is not a person, or else that arms and legs are not necessary."

"How you professional philosophers go on, Socrates! Of course I did not mean arms and legs exactly."

"I apologize, Antiphon; for I thought that you meant what you said. But what did you mean?"

"I meant, like ourselves in a more general way; able to talk and feel pain and so on."

"So dumb and paralyzed people are not people, in your view?"

"Really, Socrates! Of course they are. All right, then,

perhaps it is not quite that, but something else about people which makes them people. Tell me, Socrates, are you a student of science fiction, as they call it?"

"No, but I am aware of what it is. It deals with other worlds than our own, does it not, and the creatures found on them?"

"Just so, and it struck me that this might be a good way of achieving precision about what a person is. For how would we tell, on some other world, whether the entities in it were things or people? The advantage of this procedure is that we can change the circumstances to suit our book; imagine the entities in any way you choose—dumb or made of stone or invisible or what you like."

"Very well, Antiphon. Let us suppose I am on the moon, and I come across some Thing and am uncertain whether to treat it as a person or not. Of course I would not know its language, if it had one, but I should do my best and say: 'O Thing, you seem very strange to me both as to your shape and your color and most other things about you. Now if you have a language of your own and are conscious and can think, then you will have wants and desires like me (though perhaps different from mine), and I will call you a person and care for your interests as for my own. But if, O Thing, you have no language, but are senseless like wood or stone, then you have no true desires or interests, and in that case you are indeed a thing and not a person at all.' That is how I should proceed. Naturally it might not answer me, but if in the course of time I could establish communication with it, then my problem would be solved. And if not, when I had tried as hard as I could, then it would be solved also, for then it would be a thing and not a person."

"I agree, Socrates. And I take back what I said just now.

For it seems plain that very few of us do, in fact, have the correct idea of what a person is. That is why many men behave as if some class of people—black men, for instance, or those of another religion, or slaves or women—were not people at all, but just things. So it is no wonder that they do not care for their interest, but just use them for their own advantage, for they do not realize that they are people."

"Either that, or they prefer not to remember, Antiphon, or perhaps a bit of both. But here at least is one fine crop we can reap. We can at least teach our young people what a person is, so that they will be able to identify those entities whose interest they must treat as equal with their own."

"Certainly; such teaching is much needed, in my view."

"And is there not also a second crop? I mean, we can teach them the arguments that show us why other people are of equal importance—the ones we considered the other day?"

"Yes."

"About the third crop, though, I am not so certain."

"What third crop is this?"

Caring for the Principle

"Well, must there not be some kind of feeling or force attached to this principle about caring for others? I mean, suppose that a man said, 'I think it right, Socrates, to care for others; you have explained to me what a person is and why it is right to care for a person's interest, and I agree with you,' but then went around behaving completely selfishly and showing no remorse whatever. What would we say then?"

"I suppose, that he was not sincere in what he said."

"Yet he might not be lying exactly, Antiphon. Such a man would honestly write the principle down as his true belief, in answer to some question in an examination, for instance, yet something would be lacking. This something I call the feeling or force—or shall we say the weight?—of the principle in his heart."

"Yes, I see."

"But how we are to give him this weight I do not know, Antiphon. It seems to be not a matter for philosophy, but for some other art or science. Perhaps it comes from habit, or from being set a good example, or from learning to love and trust people, or from some other source. But in any case, these are matters of fact and not of philosophy, so we must leave them to other experts."

"Very well, Socrates. But tell me, do you usually walk around with your eyes closed?"

"What is this, Antiphon? Help me, Cephalus!"

"I see that my son has picked up some of your own methods, Socrates. I shall not help you; let us see how you behave under fire."

"Very well, I will answer. No, Antiphon, I do not."

"You need to be able to perceive how the land lies, I suppose?"

"Of course."

"Morality is not the same as land surveying, is it?"

"Hardly."

The Need to Know Facts

"What then will the man who is interested in morality want to perceive, since it is not the lie of the land? Will he want to perceive nothing at all?"

"Surely not, but I am uncertain what he will want to perceive."

"Come, come, Socrates! Pull yourself together. Morality is about the satisfaction of the interests of people, is it not?"

"Yes."

"Then is it not obvious that he will want to perceive and know about those things which chiefly affect people and their interests? And I think I can reap two crops here, at least."

"How two?"

"Well, there will be facts about the world which he will want to know; I mean, about health and safety and things of that kind which affect human beings as they now are (they might be different, of course, for Moonmen). That is one crop. But also, and perhaps more importantly, he will want to know about his own and other people's feelings and emotions and desires, for these are the very stuff out of which the satisfaction of interests is made, are they not?"

"I suppose so."

"Do not 'suppose,' Socrates, but answer up cheerfully like a good boy. I mean that a man would be a bad satisfier of interests if he never knew when someone was angry, or jealous, or frightened (and so on), wouldn't he?"

"Yes, he would."

"That's better, Socrates. So then it seems that we have these two other crops in our storehouse. There must be ways of teaching young people these two things—the knowledge of facts about the world, and the knowledge of facts about people's feelings and emotions."

"Well, Antiphon, I am amazed at your sagacity. Cephalus will say the same, I am sure."

"Certainly, Socrates. But I can see other crops also which can be reaped."

"Spare me for now, Cephalus! For the storehouse of my poor head is already overflowing and likely to burst. You would not like to see my brains boil over like porridge, would you? Well, then, let us leave it till another day."

* * *

Next morning I saw that Cephalus was all bursting with enthusiasm to speak, as if he had something very important to say; so I said to him:

"I see that you wish to speak first, Cephalus, so go ahead. But take it easy, please; I am not a Megalote, you know."

"Megalote? What is that? You mean Megarian, or Megalopolitan, or something of that sort."

"No, indeed, but Megalote. They are a strange tribe of barbarians (curiously omitted by Herodotus in his history) with enormous ears, as indeed their name implies. They can listen to many people talking at once and catch all their different views—probably they would make very good politicians. But if they are bored, they simply wrap their ears round them and go to sleep."

"Well, Socrates, I shall not bore you, I am sure. For I have it all worked out beforehand. May I then continue?"

"Of course."

The Need for Alertness or Determination

"Very well. I want you first to note, Socrates and Antiphon, that hitherto we have reaped one kind of crop only for our young men—that which is concerned with thinking and judging. We have talked of having the right idea of a person, and of the moral importance of the interests of people, and the need to be able to identify their emotions and what hurts and helps them.

"I do not deny that all this is important for them to learn, but what of their actual deeds? Do we not very often see men knowing what is right, but doing the opposite? So must there not be other things which they need besides the ones we have given them? I think that there must, and that they are as follows:

"First, they must be alert and wakeful, not wrapped up in themselves like Socrates' Megalotes when they are bored; not drugged or drunk or heedless of the world around them. Second, they must be willing, not just to have the abilities and knowledge mentioned by Socrates earlier, but to use them or bring them to bear. Otherwise they will be like men equipped with spears and swords and other weapons, but unwilling to use them—and a fat lot of good they would be in a fight! Third, they must use them in such a way as to reach a definite and determined conclusion about what they ought to do. I do not mean just in principle or vaguely, but by way of committing themselves to action on the spot, like brave hoplites who actually undertake the charge rather than just thinking that a charge should be made. And fourth and last, they must have the power actually to do what they have decided; not start the charge and then be unable to carry on with it for lack of patience or determination or any other thing.

The Value of Religion

"I have put this in 'humanist' terms, Socrates and Antiphon, because I know that we are speaking for all men, not just for those who believe in the gods. But I cannot refrain from pointing out that here, surely, is an important place for religion. Belief in the gods encourages men to do all these four things, even if it does not give them a sound logical basis. By prayer, and the imagination of a heavenly reward, and conscience, and all the other things of religion, a man is enabled to fight the good fight like a brave hoplite. Now, have I spoken well?"

"Excellent, Cephalus! Antiphon and I are still reeling under the impact of your charge. I agree with all you say, and you have set out the four requirements very clearly. About religion, though, I am not sure; I incline to think that we should leave that to the experts."

"But why? Surely it is obvious that religion helps men in the way I said."

"Not so obvious as all that, Cephalus. Have you not heard of the fat man of Crete?"

"Is this a joke like the Megalotes, Socrates?"

"Not at all; it is a true story. This Cretan was very fat, and wished to lose weight. So he consulted the oracle, and the oracle told him that there was a very rare herb, which grew only on the top of Mount Ida in Crete. If he went and ate that herb from time to time (said the oracle) it would make him lose weight. Indeed, so that he could remember the advice, the oracle cast it for him in the form of a distich, thus:

'Go to Mount Ida for your dinner:

Getting the herb will make you thinner'—

a rather vulgar couplet, but then he was a rather vulgar man, and the oracle accommodates its style to its audience."

"Well, and what happened?"

"The man obeyed the oracle, and kept constantly climbing up and down Mount Ida, looking for the herb, and eating it when he could find it; and of course, what with taking so much exercise and missing his usual food, he rapidly lost weight. It was not the herb, of course—which was in all respects quite ordinary—but the exercise. Indeed he himself came to realize this later, and accused the oracle of falsehood. But the oracle cleared itself easily—for the words were 'getting the herb,' not 'eating the herb.'"

"I still do not see what this has to do with religion."

Religion As an Incentive

"Well, Cephalus, it is quite possible that the real power of religion does not lie in its religiousness (if I may coin a word), but elsewhere. Perhaps it is the discipline and inspiration and incentive that are important, not so much the actual beliefs about the gods; just as it was the exercise that helped the fat man, not the herb. Perhaps indeed it does not matter very much what a man believes, so long as he is encouraged somehow to pursue the good life in the way that we have been talking about."

"I think that is rather muddled, Socrates; can you explain more?"

"Yes, you are right, it is muddled, for obviously different beliefs will encourage a man to do different things, not all of which may be in accordance with our principles. But what I mean is this: Suppose we persuade the young men to accept our principles, including those which you have just listed, Cephalus. They are to believe in other people's interest, know what they feel and what hurts and help them, and they are to have the alertness and determination and powers of decision making required to turn these into action. Now, I myself am willing to use any methods which produce these qualities in the young, and if a young man says that he is alert or brave 'because he is inspired by Zeus,' or 'because the words of Marx encourage him,' or even 'because he is exalted by the thought of his grandmother's cat,' I shall not mind much—provided, of course, that Zeus or Marx or the cat do not interfere with our principles in other ways."

"Yes, I see. But does Antiphon agree with us?"

Religion May Be Useful

"Certainly I agree, father. But I think you will find, Socrates, that once this truth about religion is recognized, men will not go in for religion any more."

"Aren't you forgetting one of our earlier conversations, Antiphon—the one about the sacred and the holy and all that?"

"Am I?"

"It seems so. Tell me, which is more to be admired and worshiped—an Olympic victor, or one of our principles—say, the one about caring for other men?"

"The principle, of course."

"Let us call it 'love' for short, shall we?"

"Very well."

"You will not mind if I were to write it with a capital L, 'Love,' will you? For after all we write our own names and the names of our cities with capital letters, and they are surely less important."

"I see where you are leading me, Socrates, but go on."

"Willingly, I hope, Antiphon. Well, then, if we make statues of Olympic victors, why should we not make statues of Love, so that simple men can see this majestic principle embodied, as it were, in marble or ivory, and treat it with the reverence it deserves? And could we not also justly sing hymns to Love, and do many of the other things that religious people do?"

"I suppose we could."

"Well, but you seem hesitant, Antiphon."

So Long As People Are Not Deceived

"I am frightened that the people may be deceived, Socrates. Will they not believe that there is really a person called Love, invisible but real, who will by some magical process help them in their difficulties? And they might go on to believe all the other nonsense about miracles and life after death and so on. For has not religion always really been a form of magic, Socrates? Primitive and fearful men people the world with gods who are made up out of their own fears and desires and wishes; they cause the lightning and earthquakes, make the crops grow, save those who worship them, punish the unbelievers, and all that sort of thing. But we know well enough that there are no such entities in the universe—or at least we have no evidence of them. Plainly, they are fictions, made up by men who cannot rest content with the world as it is, so that they must invent a supernatural world which seems to them more satisfactory."

"These are grave matters, Antiphon, and, though I am sure that there is a lot in what you say, I do not think this need prevent us from dressing up our principles in the grandest possible clothes. And if simple people are likely to be deceived by our statues of Love and so forth, I can explain to them, saying: 'O simple men, Antiphon here thinks that you may be deceived into supposing that this block of marble and ivory is actually a person, called Love.

I myself do not think it likely, for you must know well enough that love is not actually made of such stuff, but is a principle which lodges in the hearts and minds of men. But, since Antiphon wishes it, and perhaps he is right, I have thought it worth while to make the point.' "

The Need for Experts

"I like the way you put it all on me, Socrates! But in any case, whether we are to make a religion of our principles or not—and I agree that we cannot now discuss this properly, since there is not time—surely you will accept that we must make every effort to hire the right experts, in order to find out what will actually produce these qualities in young people?"

"Yes, Antiphon, of course I accept that. It is, though, an immensely difficult matter, and we must not expect to advance too quickly; particularly since many experts will be needed, of different kinds."

"How do you mean?"

"Well, I suppose that some of these qualities are learned (or not learned) at a very early age, and depend very much on the individual concerned. So we shall need experts in this field—'individual psychology,' I think it is called. Then again, some will be learned when our young men mix in groups with each other, so that we need experts who are able to tell us the different effects that pertain there—these are termed 'social psychologists.' Again, I suppose that the kind of society we have in Athens as a whole is important; I mean, the sort of public and economic life that goes on for all the citizens. The experts here are called 'sociologists,' I understand. We shall need all these and more besides, for surely poetry and music and painting and all the other arts have some relevance to the acquiring of our principles, do they not?"

"They do."

"It is true that many of the experts do not seem to earn their money—I have heard this, at least, of the sociologists, and I dare say it is true of others also. But then we must make sure to bring in those who are best in their field."

"Yes, we must."

"It does not much matter what they are called, after all; what we want is those men who have made a special study of the influences of young people, whether from the family or from their friends or from society as a whole, or indeed from quite other sources. There must be some such men."

"Of course there are, but I am not qualified to say just who, since I have not read very widely about such things."

"That is both just and modest, Antiphon; would that all other men were the same! For I have heard quite ignorant people, who have either not attended the academy at all or else have performed rather poorly in it, voice very confident opinions on these subjects. I have heard such men as Freud and Marx and others sometimes worshiped as gods, and at other times execrated as devils—usually by people who have not even read them properly!"

"Well, Socrates, that is characteristic of ignorant people, to praise or decry what they do not know. But now, I fear, it is time for me and Cephalus to leave you. Until tomorrow."

* * *

When I arrived on the next day, Cephalus immediately jumped up and said:

"What are you going to do about all those beautiful women, Socrates?"

"Beautiful women? Whatever do you mean? I do not have time for such delights. I am only a poor old hard-working philosopher, and must leave that sort of thing to you rich farmers."

The Virtues Again

"How forgetful you are, Socrates! I mean the lady Virtues, whom you were telling us about the other day."

"Now I remember. But did we not say that I could not woo them all, since they would conflict with each other? I have been trying to see how I could fit them all in, but no plan seems to work. For instance, I could allot each a separate day of the week, but that will not do, since there are times when a man needs more than one for the performance of some task. For instance, in bringing up children one needs kindness and wisdom together, and also justice and many others. Then again, we say sometimes that 'justice must be tempered with mercy'; but in what proportions, and do we need the lady Temperance to make the mixture for us? Personally I find Wisdom the most attractive of them all, but I am aware that even she cannot stand alone."

"Well, Socrates, but can't you find something for them to do? For they will be angry with you, I think, if you dismiss them altogether. Besides, their names are very well known in our city, and people will think you are not serious if you do not allot them some task. Am I to make a public proclamation in the marketplace, and say: 'Men of Athens, you need no longer bother about the Virtues and have no more use for words such as "courage" and "justice" and "kindness" and so on, for Socrates has convinced me that they are of no value—or, at least, he is not sure how they can be fitted into our city. Perhaps they had better be stored in a cave under the Acropolis, along with the scenery for last year's plays.' Am I to say that?"

"No, by the gods! I see that I must go further into the matter. Have you any ideas, Antiphon?"

"One thing occurs to me, Socrates, that may be of some help."

"And what is that?"

True and False Virtues

"Were these Virtues that appeared to you the true Virtues, or were they the imitations that are current in our city at this time?"

"How do you mean?"

"Well, I am only picking up the point you taught me earlier about obedience and the divine law, and all that. Was Obedience, in fact, one of those that came into your dreams?"

"She was, I remember particularly, because she kept insisting that I should obey her and not the other goddesses."

"It sounds to me as if these were not true Virtues at all, but only their fashionable counterparts or imitations. But now answer me, Socrates, is it good that a man should be obedient?"

"Yes, provided that he obeys the right things."

"And that a man should follow some rules about property and communicating with his fellowmen—let us call these honesty and truthfulness, shall we?"

"Yes, though it is not easy to say what rules exactly."

"And that he should have courage—even though we might disagree about what dangers he should face and overcome, nevertheless there will always be some dangers he ought to overcome, so that courage will be a necessity for him?"

"Yes."

"Well, then, that is what I mean by true Virtues. In Athens, and no doubt in all other places and times, there are false, immodest Virtues who say more than they ought. They are always telling us precisely what to obey, and what rules about property and communication to follow, and what to be brave about. But the true Virtues are less forward."

"And what do the true Virtues say, if anything?"

"They do not say much, Socrates. Their task is more like that of statues, who stand over various branches and departments of life, to remind us of what we are likely to need in each department. For instance, we are most likely to need courage on the battlefield, are we not?"

"Yes."

The Use of the Virtues

"We can say that without denying that we might, conceivably, need other virtues besides—for instance, justice, for I suppose it ought to occur to a Persian, even on the battlefield, that he has no business to be there at all, invading the land of Greece which does not belong to him and generally causing trouble. He ought even then to realize that he is behaving unjustly and would be better off back home in Persia making carpets, or whatever it is that Persians do. But let us assume, anyway, that the young men we are setting out to teach have made all their decisions beforehand, using those principles and abilities we listed the other day, so that they know that they are doing right—well, there they are on the battlefield and all they really need is courage."

"Yes, I see that."

"So, then, we need Courage to stand there in the line of battle—whether as a statue, or a war cry, or just as an idea in our minds—to remind us of what we need. And the same in other cases. In the law courts or in buying and selling in the marketplace, there are statues of Justice and Fair Dealing, and in some cases we may need more than one statue—for instance, I was at a party the other night where the host set two figures on the mantelpiece, one of Gaiety or Cheerfulness and the other of Temperance. For he thought, and rightly, that in this context of life—that is, a drinking-party—we had need of both."

"Then, we are to imagine the true Virtues as saying something like, 'Young men, I know that you have worked out everything carefully, according to the principles that you have learned, and that you have those qualities of alertness and resolution and so on which are needed for action, so that if all goes well you will be able to think and act rightly at all times. Nevertheless, different contexts of living have different temptations attached to them, and there are separate Vices which may overtake you in each. These are our ugly sisters, who live in the underworld and are always trying to change places with us. So we think it helpful if we stand here, one in each department, and simply suggest to you that you may have need of us'— would that be the sort of speech they would make?"

"Just so, Socrates, and I think that all the true Virtues

will have a place to stand in. It is the fashionable imitations we have to watch out for."

"But how do these arise, and how may we recognize them, Antiphon?"

"They are nourished, I think, by those men in a city who become particularly alarmed by one of the ugly sisters, the Vices, and then, instead of simply directing our attention to the true Virtues, they make up an imitation and over-feed her until she becomes gross and overweening."

"Please give me an example."

"Well, when drunkenness was rife in our city in the old days, and men neglected Temperance, there were those who were so alarmed by this drunkenness that they in-vented a false Temperance, whose orders (they claimed) were that men should not drink at all, even in moderation."

"How absurd!"

"Certainly, but many people followed them. And then what happens is that the younger generation, rightly per-ceiving that this imitation Temperance is no true Virtue at all, wrongly conclude that there is no such thing as true Temperance and believe that all the Virtues and Vices are simply the invention of adults, designed to keep young people in their place. I say this with authority, for that is what I myself was inclined to believe until recently."

"And does this apply to all the Virtues?"

The Need for More Study

"I think so, though I am not at all sure how many of them there are, or what names they ought to have."

"What! Are they not already named and numbered and

registered in the state archives? I thought at least that they must pay income tax and have their personal details filed with the local authorities, for if not, then so far as the state is concerned they might as well not exist at all."

"You will have your joke, Socrates, but I intend something serious. For instance, we have a word for a man who respects the property of others, do we not?"

"Yes, we call him 'honest.'"

"And for one who does not tell lies?"

"Him we call 'truthful.'"

"And for the man who respects his neighbor's life and person and does not commit murder or assault upon him?"

"Yes, we call him—well, the word we use is—good heavens, Antiphon, I do not know what the word is!"

"There is none in our language, Socrates; though for all I know perhaps the Scythians or the Agathyrsoi have a word for it, as the saying goes. Yet this is surely a most important virtue, more important anyway than not stealing or lying."

"Yes, indeed."

"So perhaps your suggestion about filing and numbering the virtues was not so comical after all. For do we not need to make a proper list of them, giving each a clear and definite name and department, at the same time making sure that each is a true Virtue and not an imitation? Until we can do that, we shall not be clear about how many there are, or in which departments of life to place them."

"Well said, Antiphon, and now if these good ladies return to me in my dreams tonight I shall know how to answer them."

"I am glad to be of service, Socrates. And now Cephalus and I will bid you au revoir (as they say in Scythia), for we are going on a journey tomorrow, and we must be up early."

"Why, where are you going?"

"We are off to Corinth. It will be an interesting journey, because I have heard that their ways there are even more free and licentious than ours here in Athens—at least so my father tells me. The people there, or some of them, are extremely worried about the effects which, they say, the plays and other spectacles are having on the young people. So I shall be able to tell you about this on our return, for I imagine that you will agree that this, too, relates to the subject of our inquiry."

"It is certainly not irrelevant. Indeed, to judge by what one hears in the marketplace, you would think that morality was chiefly concerned with sex and violence—not, indeed, that these two things are unimportant. So I will be only too pleased to consider what you have to tell me on your return. Have a good journey, the two of you!"

CHAPTER 5

The Methods of Art

When I arrived at Cephalus' house about two weeks
later, I was surprised to see, not only him and his son
Antiphon, but also two friends of mine with whom I had
had many conversations in the past—Adeimantus and
Thrasymachus. Cephalus and Antiphon were going over
the accounts of their estate, sitting together and talking
quietly, and Thrasymachus was prowling up and down
like a wolf, muttering to himself darkly, and evidently in-
tent upon his own thoughts. I did not wish to disturb
them, but my old friend Adeimantus, on the other hand,
was sitting by himself in a relaxed sort of way, reading a
letter and chuckling to himself. So I went up to him and
said:

"Good morning, Adeimantus, and what are you
reading?"

"I have a letter from an old schoolmaster, who has been
telling his pupils that story of Bellerophon—how by his
virtue and courage he slew the terrible Chimaira, which (as

you remember, Socrates) had 'a lion's head, a snake's tail, and a goat's middle.'"

"A noble story, encouraging our youth to valor and goodness."

"For some, yes, but this schoolmaster writes to me of several pupils who were offended with Bellerophon's deed, because (they said) they were so fond of animals. It seems that these pupils belong to a club which is very popular in our city, for the preservation of wild beasts of all kinds. According to them, Bellerophon should not have killed this monster but ought to have reported its existence to the proper authorities, who would have looked after it until it died of old age or by some other natural event."

"By the gods, Adeimantus, a strange set of young people we have nowadays!"

"We have indeed, Socrates, and it makes me wonder whether what we said in our earlier conversation was altogether correct."

"About what in particular?"

Should Writers and Artists Only Represent the Good?

"I mean (if you remember) when we said that authors ought to represent nothing bad in their books and plays, but only what is virtuous and good."

"Surely we cannot go back on that conclusion?"

"You yourself have said, Socrates, that we must follow 'wheresoever the argument may lead us,' and if we were wrong or over-hasty, must we not make every endeavor to correct ourselves? For this is no trivial matter but concerns the whole education and well-being of our young people."

"Certainly."

"Very well, then. Shall I set my doubts in order, one

after the other or shall I mix them all up together higgledy-piggledy, as in the speeches of our politicians?"

"No, by Zeus, not as with the politicians. For (as it seems to me at any rate) they are not so much concerned with truth but with capturing the votes of the populace on the one hand, or with their own prejudices and emotions on the other. Whereas we, I take it, are concerned with the truth—we do not think we know everything already but are willing to learn and discuss with each other like rational men, not like the baboons of Libya."

"This opinion of yours, Socrates, may get you into trouble with the authorities one day. But I agree as to our own procedure. First, then, it seems to me impossible to represent only the good and not the bad at all."

"How so?"

Is It Possible To Do So?

"I mean this: Things are not just hot, are they, or high, except by contrast with what is less hot or less high—that is, with the cold or the low?"

"Of course."

"And so with everything else; we cannot have a true idea of what is skillful or straight or beautiful or heavy unless we also have an idea of what is clumsy or crooked or ugly or light?"

"Yes."

"Then this will apply to the good also. Surely our young people cannot understand good men represented as doing good things unless they also understand the opposite. Moreover, Socrates, do not many of our best writers show good men behaving well in the face of evil—overcoming monsters and criminals, suffering at the hands of wicked men, and so forth? Are these not intended to praise virtue by contrasting it with vice?"

"It seems so, certainly."

"Then apparently, as with my schoolmaster's story about Bellerophon, much will depend not on the tale itself but on how it is received by the young."

"How do you mean?"

The Bible

"Well, I have heard a story about the son of a god who came down to earth in order to help mankind. In this story—and very plausible it is too—this man (or perhaps we should call him a god) was betrayed by a friend of his to the authorities. The authorities then had him falsely accused and condemned to death, although he was innocent; he was tortured and finally killed by being nailed to a piece of wood."

"A horrible story, and not fit for the ears of anybody, particularly the young."

"So I thought, Socrates. Yet those who believe this story among the barbarians have written it down in a book, which they value highly and count as sacred, and they make all their young people read it diligently. When I questioned them about this, they replied, first, that the story was true and important and that young people ought to be told what was true; and second, that the very horrors of the story would encourage the young to resent injustice and count the man who died as a hero. That is what I mean by saying that much will depend on how our stories are received by the young."

"That seems certainly true, and perhaps we were too simple, being like young children ourselves, in labeling stories 'good' and 'bad'—as if they were like milk and cheese, either fresh or curdled."

The Use of Representing the Bad

"My second doubt, Socrates, was about whether we were right in dismissing representations of the bad and the diseased as casually as we did before."

"Well, Adeimantus, I agree that we may need the bad as a contrast with the good, so that the good may shine more brightly—just as the moon is visible only in the dark. But surely we do not need the bad for any other purpose?"

"In our earlier talk, Socrates, we said that the bad was like disease, and that we wanted our young people to be healthy?"

"Yes, and surely that was correct."

"Certainly. But tell me, does the serious and virtuous man think himself to be perfect?"

"Certainly not."

"Then he will, in some degree, have disease in his soul?"

"Yes."

"He will recognize this and seek to cure it?"

"Of course; otherwise he would not be virtuous."

"And will not a large part of the cure lie in his own hands? I mean, he cannot rely entirely on expert doctors of the soul, who will tell him simply to take certain medicines. He will have to understand his own disease properly and do everything in his power to remedy it."

"Yes."

"Then he will need to know, will he not, what diseases the soul may have and from what causes they arise, and he will, I think, find it useful to have representations of these, so that he may see his own soul as in a mirror—just as ordinary doctors need pictures and other representations of physical diseases in order that they may learn about them and how to cure them. Indeed I have a young friend, Theophrastus, who intends to write a book setting out various characters, mostly bad, so that, as he says, 'our sons will prove to be better men if we give them reminders of these characters.'"

Imitation

"But is there not a danger, Adeimantus, that they will imitate these bad characters?"

"I do not dispute that, Socrates. And this may remind us that much may depend not only (as we said earlier) on how the young people receive such representations but also on the manner in which we present them to the young; I mean, whether we present them as things to be imitated, or things to be avoided, or in some other manner."

"What other manner could there be?"

"Here we come to my third doubt, Socrates, which is perhaps more serious than the first two; just as, you know, experienced generals sometimes put their most serious and powerful fighters in the third line of hoplites, so that even if the first two lines are defeated the third may stand fast and maintain the battle-line."

"Well, and what is this third line of troops? I already tremble at the onslaught."

The Nature of the Arts

"I fear that perhaps we have been thinking about the whole matter in quite the wrong way. We have not been thinking about what poets and dramatists and other writers say in accordance with the art they have, but in accordance with some other art."

"I do not understand you at all, Adeimantus."

"Well, then: Is the figure 8 a pleasing shape?"

"Some may think so."

"But suppose that a child, asked to add 3 and 3, gave us this figure 8 as an answer; would that be a good or bad answer?"

"Bad, of course."

"And yet the 8 may be a good figure?"

"Yes."

"So then it appears that there is one art, mathematics, which the child does not understand, but perhaps he understands another art and puts the first 3 next to the second 3 (having turned one of them around) and joins them together to make an 8, which is a pleasing figure."

"Let us suppose so."

"And is it not the same with all the other arts? I mean, if somebody were to answer questions of science by throwing dice, or questions of music by the art of medicine, and so on—would we not think that he had lost his way among the arts and sciences?"

"We would."

"Now, Homer is considered a better poet than you or I, isn't he?"

"Of course."

"And Ictinus who built the Parthenon, a better builder?"

"Yes."

"So some poets and builders are better than others? And I suppose we must say the same as regards dramatists and painters and musicians—and even of those who show their citizens various scenes and happenings viewed from afar?"

"What is this last thing, Adeimantus?"

"Well, Socrates. I have heard that among the Hyperboreans (where they have men who are either very skilled, or else expert magicians—I do not know which), many citizens have a kind of box, and when they press knobs on this it shows them all kinds of wonderful scenes and dramas, just as if they were at the Panathea."

"Good heavens! But it makes no difference to the argument."

"No, indeed. Tell me, then, in virtue of what do we call something better or worse in respect of these kinds of arts? I mean this: Is a painting good because it is a painting of a horse? Or is a play or poem good because it deals with one sort of person rather than another?"

"No, but for some other reason."

"It seems, Socrates, from what you have admitted about the horse—and all the other examples with which I will not weary you—that goodness in poetry and painting and the other arts does not consist in *what* is represented at all, but in something else—perhaps in whether the representation is done well or badly. Thus we could have a *good* painting of a bad horse, could we not?"

"I suppose so."

What Literature Does

"Well, then, that is what I meant by saying that we had been thinking about this in quite the wrong way. If we had stuck by what we said in our earlier conversation and wished to prohibit all representations of what was bad, let us imagine what a poet or dramatist might say to us. 'O Socrates and Adeimantus,' he might say, 'I understand you well enough. You do not wish our young people corrupted by what is bad. But you do not seem to understand me at all. For the nature of my art is this: to show people their own souls, and the souls of them around them, in such a way that they will not only take pleasure in seeing what I show but also gain a kind of understanding and knowledge of it. If I practice my art well, like Homer, they will come to understand what anger is like by hearing my verse about Achilles; what grief is like, hearing about Andromache, and so on. I am in my own way a kind of teacher of the soul, but I do it, not by philosophy—I am not clever, as you two philosophers are—but by a gift which the Muses have given me and also by long study of the hearts of men. Surely, at least I am not to be blamed if some man uses a knife to kill another. In a word, my art is not intended to show something for people to imitate, but rather—as you yourselves have said—it holds up a sort of mirror to the soul. If, indeed, I were to preach at our young people, saying to them, "Do this" or "Imitate such-and-such a man," you would be right to turn upon me like wolfhounds and say, "O poet, now it is you who have become muddled about the nature of the various arts. It is we, the philosophers, whose job it is to preach virtue directly in this way; your job is to help men understand both virtue and vice by your own particular art." But now, as it is, I do not infringe on your prerogatives, so it is only fair that you should not infringe on mine.' Might the poet or dramatist, or any other such, reasonably say something like that to us?"

"It seems that he might. But, Adeimantus, I am now myself in doubt."

"What about, Socrates?"

Imitation Again

"Well, it seems to me that you and your poet have distinguished the nature of these two arts (if indeed there are only two kinds) clearly; that is, the mirror-holding art of the poet and the dramatist on the one hand, and the art of those who wish to hold up to our young people, not a mirror, but examples of good things to imitate—the preacher's art, if you like. But might not our young people fail to distinguish these, as we have done?"

"I suppose they might."

"So that, when the poet or the dramatist shows them Polyphemus being cruel to Odysseus, or Clytemnestra murdering her husband, or other such wicked actions—intending, of course, not to recommend such behavior but only to show its nature—might not some young man or girl want to imitate these people?"

"Perhaps."

"It was fear of this, I think, which led us to a wrong conclusion in our earlier conversation; in that, we wished to banish all of this kind of art but also all knowledge of bad actions and people, both present and past."

"Surely an impossible task and an unnecessary one, Adeimantus. What we must do, as you mentioned before, is to instill some understanding into the young about these two arts, so that they will receive each in the right manner. In particular—since imitation seems to be a natural thing and has no need of teaching—we must make them understand the arts of the poets and other writers. We must show them that these arts are not for pleasure only, nor for imitation, but for gaining a certain kind of understanding which is important for virtue. Little by little, from their earliest years, we must acquaint them with good examples of these arts; I mean, 'good' in respect of the arts themselves, not examples which imitate or represent virtue—just as you were now saying, about a good painting of a horse being different from a good horse. . . ."

At this point I noticed that Cephalus and Thrasymachus, who had been listening intently, were becoming very excited and wished to speak. At first both began to speak together, until I restrained them with gentle words, and then Cephalus burst out:

Cephalus' Feelings

"Really, Socrates, and you too, Adeimantus, I cannot sit here while you discuss this in your clever philosophical way. I do not wish to boast, but I am a good Greek gentleman, as my fathers were, and I know right from wrong without the help of philosophers. Surely there are some things which no poet or writer should portray, whether they are 'holding up a mirror to the soul' or anything else. Indeed in Sparta there are excellent laws about such things, and in my opinion it is about time that the Athenians adopted such laws. For already our young people are being corrupted with shows and spectacles and cheap books of all kinds, representing the most lewd and disgusting things. Indeed, I would not be surprised if those who write these books were bribed with Persian gold in order that our country should become an easy prey to foreign invaders. Why, I saw in the marketplace only yesterday a story in which—if you can believe me—a free-born Athenian housewife, married (in the story) to a respectable citizen, was represented as walking around the town by herself, without even a slave to accompany her! Worse, she was dressed like a barbarian, and it was possible for the men of the town to see her knees! I apologize for mentioning such revolting things, Socrates, in order to make myself clear, but surely there are some things which are so

monstrous and contrary to nature that we must prohibit
them, and. . . ."

Thrasymachus' Criticism

Here Thrasymachus could not restrain himself any
longer, and interrupted in a very sarcastic manner:
"Are you a god, Cephalus, or descended from gods?"
"Of course not, Thrasymachus; why do you ask such a
silly question?"
"Because I thought that you must have ichor, not blood,
in your veins; and feed on nectar and ambrosia, not on
ordinary food like us poor mortals. And I imagined that
you were not born of an ordinary woman, by the natural
process of childbirth, and that you never excreted or in-
dulged in any other such natural activity. For it seems that
you count this sort of thing, in your own words, as 'contrary to nature,' so that your own nature and that of your
family must be something very divine and remarkable."
"Not at all, Thrasymachus. But the things you mention
are disgusting and ought not to be talked of, much less
represented in poetry and literature."
"There you are, Socrates! Now you can see what my
friends and I are fighting against! For many years these
old men have been suppressing the natural desires of us
young people, and it is our duty now to make as much of
these desires as possible. Particularly in relation to anger
and in sexual matters we feel it right to represent these as
forcefully and vividly as we can, both in literature and on
the stage. I do not care about 'the kind of arts that poets
and dramatists have,' as you call it; I want to show the
citizens what Cephalus here would call the 'nasty' side of

life and to shock them with it. I should like to show them men and women doing such things as. . . ."

Here Cephalus became very alarmed and angry, so that I was obliged to intervene, in order that the conversation could continue. So I said:

Socrates Intervenes

"O Cephalus and Thrasymachus, I know you to be friends of mine, and I know also that you are not like barbarians or politicians, who prefer to make long emotional speeches at each other, rather than asking and answering questions in the way that civilized people do. Please, therefore, let us all keep calm, and see whether what you have both said is true or not. Perhaps I can begin by asking Thrasymachus this: You say, Thrasymachus, if I understand you, that in sexual and other such matters there is nothing particularly nasty or disgusting?"

"Certainly not."

"They are just like anything else, quite ordinary? I mean, they are like tables or beds, or bits of mud, or sticks of wood, or anything else one might think of?"

"Yes."

"Now you wish the stories and plays which you and your friends write to be good of their kind?"

"Of course."

"A story is not good, is it, just because it is about a table or a bit of mud?"

"No."

"Then I think that you fail to do yourself and your friends justice, my friend. For by your own account it is not what your stories are *about* which makes them good. You may write stories dealing with the lewdest subjects and shock Cephalus and his friends until they pass laws like the Spartans, but that will not make your stories good. It seems to me, Thrasymachus, that you are not really interested in good stories at all, but in advocating some way of life, advising men to cultivate Aphrodite and Ares at the expense of the other gods or something of that kind. Do you not think so, Cephalus?"

"You are quite right, Socrates. Thrasymachus here is out to change our morality. For he will not only write stories, but demonstrate such acts in public or draw pictures of them on walls. He is a moralist (though of the worst possible kind) and not concerned with the arts at all."

"And yet, Cephalus, is not that true of you also?"

"What?"

"Well, look at it like this. Are there not things which are more bad and disgusting than those which Thrasymachus represents?"

"How so?"

"I mean, such things as battles, in which many men die and are wounded, or when Polyphemus eats Odysseus' companions, or the story we spoke of earlier, about an innocent man who was unjustly accused and condemned and killed? Are not those worse than Thrasymachus' examples of sexual behavior?"

"I suppose they are worse."

"Then surely they ought not to be represented in our poems and plays."

Not What Is Represented, but How

"But, Socrates, it all depends on how the representation is done. If the poet or dramatist is good at his art, he will portray even these terrible things in a way which gives pleasure, and adds to them a kind of nobility, or at least a kind of interest and awareness—I do not know how to describe it exactly—from which the audience may learn."

"Well done, Cephalus! Now it seems that you are saying what we said before. For we said, as you remember, that *what* was represented did not make the art good or bad, but *how* it was represented—whether with skill and insight, or in a way which was boring and dull and told us nothing new or interesting. If we are all agreed on that, perhaps we can make progress in our conversation. And now tell me, Adeimantus—for I look to be instructed by you—how would you judge about all this? I mean, about the stories of Bellerophon and Polyphemus, and Thrasymachus' tales, and all the other things we have heard of?"

"I should say, Socrates, first of all, that this is a long and difficult business and that we need the help of all the wise and experienced men we can get hold of. Above all, we need a clearer understanding of the many different ways in which it is possible that our young people should be affected. About one of these we are perhaps partly clear already."

"Which do you mean?"

"I mean that which we have mentioned several times— whether a poem or play is good in its own category; that is, whether it is good *as* a poem or play, and never mind what it represents. If we are concerned with the *education* of the young, rather than simply with stuffing them full of good food as their mothers do, this will be very important. For this art plainly contributes much towards their understanding of human nature, and education depends on understanding."

"Granted, but what else?"

"We must then find out whether the mere representation of something—say, of some sexual or violent activity—makes young people wish to imitate it."

"Surely we can take that for granted."

Possible Effects of Art

"Not at all; remember the barbarian story of the unjust man condemned to death. Perhaps the representation will have the effect of turning the young away from such things, rather than towards them. Or perhaps, as I believe the young Aristotle says, seeing representations of terrible or bad things will have the effect of purging the soul so that those who see them will be less inclined to act in this way—they will have had, as it were, a kind of second-hand pleasure in such representations and not feel so strongly impelled to engage in such activities in their everyday lives. And this (if it is true) would be a great gain."

"I am not sure I follow you."

"Well, if a person is very angry or violent, for example, he may perhaps purge this anger and violence from his soul by watching a play in which anger and violence are represented, and so he would not wish to be angry or violent with his neighbors or in the marketplace. Moreover, he would perhaps be happier in himself, feeling less angry and calmer, somewhat as if he had had a dream or a daydream or a fantasy which made him feel happier and less inclined to treat the world as an enemy."

"That might sometimes be true."

"Yes, Socrates, but we do not know whether it is true of some young people, or of none, or of all. Moreover, even this is likely to be too simple."

"I see that we have more work to do, and that you do not let us off lightly."

"No, by the gods; how could it be an easy matter since we are dealing with the human soul, which as we know is much more complicated even than the body—and that is complicated enough!"

"Very well; proceed."

"It may well be, Socrates, that young people will imitate certain aspects of what is represented, but not others. For instance, they might admire and imitate Bellerophon's dress, or the way he speaks, but not his courage; or, if they do not imitate things in the story but rather use them as daydreams, maybe they will daydream about one element in the story but not about another. Or perhaps our young girls will be affected in one way but our young men in quite a different way. Or, again, perhaps it depends on the age of the young people, or upon their families, or many other things."

"All this makes me wonder whether we have anything definite to say at all, Adeimantus."

"Do not despair, Socrates; even to become clear about the problem is of great importance. I am sure we are both wearied with the common run of men in the assembly—not only the politicians, but anyone else who thinks himself able to pronounce on such matters without taking thought—who tell us to do this and that with great violence and persuasiveness. Something sensible can be said, but not easily."

The Need for More Research

"What, then, shall we ask our wise men to do in helping us with these problems, Adeimantus?"

"We shall ask them first of all to keep firmly in mind the categories we have mentioned. They can begin, at least, by telling us what poems and plays and stories are good within their own category, as we explained, and which are suitable for young people of various ages, so that they may learn something of this art and gain the understanding which it provides. This should not be too difficult. As for the rest, I think we need much more knowledge than we have."

"How do you mean?"

"I mean this; that if we are concerned, not with good poems and plays as such, but with which ones will inspire to virtue, or be imitated, or have some effect of this kind, then we need to discover this by experiment. For a great deal will depend on the nature of young people and how they receive and react to these things, and this we do not know. With the poems and plays that are good in themselves, we do not have this problem, for here we can introduce young people to this art, as to mathematics or science or philosophy or any other art which has its own standards of goodness contained within it. But if we are concerned with other effects, it is more difficult."

"Yes, I see."

"Then do you also see this, Socrates, that it is the height of folly to pretend to know when you do not know? We have just seen, haven't we, that the effects of the story of Bellerophon and the barbarian story about the man unjustly condemned and tortured may be quite different from what we had thought. So, then, until we can show clearly what effects various stories have, and upon whom, and at what times, and under what conditions, we cannot claim to know anything."

"No, we can't."

"But with poems and stories that are good in their own right we have some knowledge. For these have been tested by many generations of men, which is the only experiment we can put them to. They are good in themselves, whatever their effects otherwise, and so we have to teach our young people to appreciate their goodness. I hope you will agree on this, Socrates, and Cephalus and Thrasymachus, too. And if we are able to avoid becoming too emotional, as our friends did just now, but rather pursue this task with diligence, then we shall soon be able to give our young people this kind of goodness at any rate, which I regard as no small thing. The other effects of which we have spoken may wait until we have knowledge of them instead of mere opinion. And now I must bid you good day for I have promised to tell my son some stories about a little girl with a red hood and a wolf, and giants and beanstalks, and many other such. Farewell."

The Obstacles to Philosophy

At this point Adeimantus left us and with him went also Thrasymachus, frowning darkly. So I turned to Cephalus and said:

"Well, Cephalus, what do you think of all that? I hope now at least you will believe me when I say that I know little or nothing and am not at all clear about these matters. For you have seen how Adeimantus has led me in the argument like a little child, showing me that things which I had thought before were not really so but only appeared to be so."

"That may be, Socrates, but I blush to think how angry I and Thrasymachus became during the discussion. It reminds me of how Antiphon and I used to quarrel, before we took up philosophy."

Here Antiphon, who had obviously grown up a great deal in the last few months, said: "That was as much my fault as yours, father. But we are somewhat improved nowadays, Socrates, are we not?"

"Certainly," I said, "but philosophy is a hard task-mistress, and I am not surprised that many people are unwilling to obey her for long. Indeed, perhaps we ought to have predicted that anger and violence would be shown in this discussion you have recounted to us, being on the subject that it was."

"How so?"

"Well, are not the demands of philosophy like those of a bright light—the sun, for instance, or some lamp that a man might kindle in a house? Most men, I think prefer to spend their time lying in the dark and dreaming, making up their own pictures of the world which they paint in whatever colors they most enjoy. When they get up, since they have no light, they naturally stumble about and curse and swear when they bump into the furniture and other things which exist but which they cannot see. A large amount of what one hears, indeed, in the world is not much more than these dreams and curses. But if some-body shows them a light, do you think that they will be grateful?"

"They ought to be, surely."

"Perhaps so, Cephalus, but they are not. For, first of all, the light hurts their eyes, which are accustomed to the darkness, so that they become angry, like a newborn child when it first sees the light of day—you know how they squall and cry and make all kinds of trouble. And second, the light reveals to them things that they had much rather not see; I mean, their own fears and follies. And besides, it shows up their dreams for what they are—fantasy, not truth. Many of these dreams, you know, are connected with sex and violence and things of that kind. So it is not surprising that, when such subjects are discussed openly in the light of philosophy they are unable to tolerate it, but prefer to close their eyes and dream once more."

"But how are we to help them, then?"

"There is no quick way, Cephalus; have you not heard the saying, 'You can lead a Spartan to a banquet, but you can't make him eat'? But it is, I think—though I should need to bring in some experts here, too—mostly a matter of establishing trust. For naturally those who dream in this way will bring real people, the men who exist in the real world, into their dreams and, as it were, put them on the stage. They will cast this man in the role of an enemy, who cannot be trusted—a bad man, tainted with evil and corruption—and that man they will cast as a friend, one like themselves, 'an officer and a gentleman' (if the dreamer is of that sort himself) on whom they can rely; another man they may feel uncertain about, not being sure whether he is good or bad."

"Yes, they do; just as in time of war or in political battles people are not accepted and trusted for what they are but are considered only as allies or enemies."

"Exactly so; or like a child who will hate one person and be passionately fond of another, not being mature enough to recognize that a person may be different from himself and yet trustworthy. The child wants everything his own way; he wishes that the world was peopled with duplicates of himself, since he cannot tolerate compromise. And this,

Cephalus, I take to be the most difficult part of philosophy and indeed of education in general—how to make men sufficiently secure and confident to be willing to learn rather than dream. But perhaps we can discuss this further tomorrow."

CHAPTER 6

Other Methods

The next day when I arrived I saw Cephalus and Antiphon discussing eagerly, so I said:

The Importance of Trust and Discussion

"Good morning, Cephalus and Antiphon! It is nice to see an example of what we were discussing yesterday, and such a shining example too."

"An example of what, Socrates? Antiphon, do you know what he means?"

"I have no idea, but doubtless he will tell us."

"That is just what I mean, Antiphon: an example of trust and learning, which you and Cephalus here are setting. Would that other men could manage to do the same!"

"We were only talking, Socrates."

"Yes, but think how many different skills and abilities, yes, and virtues too, are involved in this!"

"How do you mean?"

"Well, let me try to list them, if you will forgive a longer speech than usual. First of all, you do not regard each other as enemies or with suspicion but as friends engaged in a common enterprise, like building a house or planning a holiday together. That is in itself a great thing. Next, you listen to what each other has to say and answer it. That sounds simple, but it is in fact very rare. Usually one person does not reply to another—he prefers his own dream to the other man's so that the two are like parallel lines which never meet, each continuing along with his own path without any regard for what the other has said. One cannot do business that way, let alone philosophy. Third, you are willing and eager, not only to listen to what is said, but to read those things which are related to the discussion. This, too, sounds simple, but many men are suspicious and frightened of things written on paper unless they are simply echoes of their own dreams. When they are given something to read they say that they 'can't understand it' or that they 'don't like the general tone of it;' by which they mean simply that they are unwilling to wake up from their dreams."

"Yes, Socrates, I understand you well enough. But can't we consider these points for the purposes of education?"

"How?"

"When I was at school, Socrates—though for Cephalus his schooldays may be more difficult to remember—I don't think that I had anyone such as you whom I could trust to the extent of being able to discuss and converse with them about life, and my own feelings, and morality, and things of that kind."

"Perhaps there were such people, Antiphon, but you did not trust them."

"Well, perhaps so, but they appeared to me always in the

role of rulers or authorities, telling us what we could and what we could not do. I did not see them ever as friends and allies in a search for truth."

Teachers Need More Power

"I understand what you mean, Antiphon. But perhaps we must not blame the schoolteachers too much; they are busy men and not very well paid for their labors. And besides, they are hedged about with a great many rules laid down by the state whereby they have to spend most of their time ensuring that their pupils are trained for the public examinations and behave in the way that their parents and the local authorities wish them to behave."

"Yes, but we must put a stop to this, Socrates. Otherwise our moral education of the young will be handicapped from the start."

"What do you suggest, then?"

"First of all, I think that the schoolteachers must be given much more power—though within limits, of course, so that they are not allowed to behave like tyrants or monsters. But they should have a freer hand to run their schools as they wish, in whatever way they think they will help the moral development of their pupils, both as regards the teaching of subjects and as regards the discipline they exercise over their pupils and their general association with them. For you know how children differ, Socrates. With one you need to be very firm and severe at times, and with others you can be more friendly—each case is different, and the schoolteacher is more likely to know of these differences than the local authorities who (however wise they may be on other matters) do not know these pupils."

"Yes, but schoolteachers are not all-wise, are they?"

"Of course not."

"Then we shall want to advise them, at least, Antiphon—if there is anything definite that we can tell them. For I must acknowledge to you that, as it seems to me, very little is really known about this subject. There is much, indeed, that people think they know, some of it being given grand titles such as 'research' or 'educational theory,' but upon examination it usually turns out either to be common knowledge already or else to be totally unproven."

"I agree, and this is surely an additional reason for leaving things, within reason, to the schoolteachers. For most of what is said and done by the state authorities has a political or social bias and is not concerned with education at all—I mean, not concerned with the acquisition of knowledge and understanding, but rather with other goods, such as social advantages or money or something of that kind. Fashion, too, plays a large part. Our schools are very different from what they were in Cephalus' time, but there is no real evidence that they are better, at least in certain respects."

"Well, then, Antiphon, do you think that nothing can be recommended to the schoolteachers?"

"I didn't say that. Indeed, I think there are many things that ought to be done by them which at present they do not do—things that they might, indeed, be eager to do if they were given time, and if the point of doing them was properly explained."

"And what things are these?"

Schools Should Be More Like Families

"No doubt they are very many, Socrates. But the first and foremost, I think, concerns this matter of trust. We must somehow arrange our schools so that they are not like factories, in which pupils and teachers work for certain hours only, but more like families."

"How do you mean?"

"Well, it is only by close association that trust can be built up between people, is it not, as in a family? I don't know, of course, but I suspect it is by sharing things together—food and drink and warmth and holidays and other such things, and of course conversation—that members of the same family are able to know and trust each other. It seems to be important that something like the same conditions should apply to schools, insofar as this is practicable."

"Yes, I see."

"So that every pupil should have, not just other pupils sitting next to him at their desks, but friends and brothers, and he should also have a father and a mother, as it were, among the schoolteachers with whom he can communicate as to his real father and mother—indeed, in some respects he might find it easier to do so, since parents and children often quarrel with each other, as Cephalus and I used to."

"But what will these family groups do together, Antiphon? Are they not somewhat artificial, since their members are not in fact related?"

"There is plenty for them to do, Socrates—and I don't only refer to the fact that they can form teams for the Olympic and other games from among their members. In the first place, they can look after themselves and their own needs, instead of being waited on by servants, for some of them, at least, will be older and well able to do all the things—or arrange for them to be done—which are now done by slaves and cooks and doorkeepers and cleaners and all those sorts of people. Second, there will be many enterprises which they can undertake: They can go on journeys together, or plan and erect some useful building, or keep a garden, or any other such thing that one can think of."

"It sounds as if you are planning a factory rather than a school after all, Antiphon! For surely the pupils are not there to erect buildings and grow onions and so on, but to learn?"

"Yes, Socrates, but these activities—besides being useful in themselves—will bind them together in friendship, as it were. They will provide a base on which learning may be built. For when they are friends, and know each other they and their schoolteachers will be able to discuss together frankly and with trust. Otherwise all of them will just go on dreaming, as you put it—for one may dream in a classroom as well as anywhere else, you know."

"Certainly."

"Moreover, there should be pupils of all ages and both sexes in this group. For it must be as far as possible like a true family, in which the older spend time helping the younger, and girls and boys work together, and so on."

"But will that not create great difficulties, Antiphon? For surely some of them, being of a different age or intelligence or state of knowledge than the others, will need to be taught together, separately from the rest? I mean, some (perhaps the younger or more stupid ones) will just be learning to read, while others who can read already will be studying literature in a more advanced way or perhaps learning a new language? And so with mathematics and science and indeed all other subjects. So where is your family then?"

"Where it always was, Socrates. Tell me, does the father of a family work in the house, alongside the wife?"

"Not usually."

"And the children, do not they spend most of their time outside the house, either at school or working elsewhere?"

"Yes."

"But they are still a family, aren't they? For they are bound together by many forms of sharing and affection. So that how much time they spend together is not the only consideration. In the same way, Socrates, I am not saying that the pupils in school should not spend a great deal of time in learning different subjects, for which they will be grouped together in the way that best fits them—I mean their state of knowledge in relation to the subject. But they will have this home or family, so to speak, at school as well. But what do you think of all this, Cephalus?"

"I see a different difficulty, Antiphon. For will not this—if it works at all—override and thrust out the pupil's real family? Why can't we rely upon ordinary families to do the work you are discussing?"

"I hope we can, to some extent, but nowadays families are often at war, or broken up, or too small for the sort of work I have been talking about. Moreover, doesn't the pupil need some kind of intermediate base between his own family and the vast outside world? I mean, somewhere which allows him something of the protection and security of a family, yet in a more extended form—a sort of halfway house, as it were. For the world is a big place, and its difficulties and responsibilities are many, so that I should not be surprised if each pupil needed some practice in them before striking out on his own."

Parents Do Not Own Children

"Well, Antiphon, I dare say you are right. So, then, first we must give more power to the schoolteachers, and then—but wait, Antiphon, are we really sure that the schoolteachers are the best people; what about the parents—after all, it is their children we are talking about."

"But parents do not own children, you know, as if they were property. We may, as it were, delegate their early upbringing to their parents as being the best and most willing teachers for that time. But thereafter we recognize that children need all that the state can give them which is best for them—whether the parents want it or not. For if the parents wanted to beat a child constantly, or denied it the right medicines for its health, would we not rightly intervene?"

"I suppose so. But I am worried that our schoolteachers may not be the best possible."

"And rightly, Cephalus; they are certainly not the best, though many of them are no doubt excellent. And is not one reason for this just what we have been saying; that is, that they are not trusted by the authorities and treated as responsible, nor given any real power? They are virtually like hired slaves, whom we use to do our dirty work for us. If they had more power and freedom from restriction, perhaps more first-rate people would enter the profession. As it is, it too often attracts the dull and respectable, who wish to earn a secure living. But we cannot attract people of vision and force unless we allow them scope for their talents."

"Very well, then; let us do as you suggest."

At this point I felt that the discussion was becoming somewhat wild, like an animal that had just been released from captivity, so I remarked:

"Cephalus, am I getting old, or what?"

"None of us is getting any younger, Socrates."

"Very true, and one day I must discuss with you whether this is a necessary truth, or could be otherwise. But now—whether it is age or something else—I feel a little lost. Not that Antiphon is mistaken, I am sure, but all these points are very general ones—they need working out in particular cases. I mean, in the schools themselves. I would like to have lunch and then raise another question—relevant indeed to this one but not the same."

"Very well; let's have lunch."

*   *   *

"Now then, Socrates, we are well fed and fortified. What is this question you would like to raise? Antiphon and I have waited long enough."

"Well, I am a little hesitant, after Antiphon's eloquent exposition of the 'school family,' as we might call it. Perhaps I could first ask Antiphon a question. What is it, Antiphon, that your schoolteachers and pupils will be learning in these families—I mean, that is specifically to do with morality?"

The "Topic" Approach to Moral Education

"I have not considered deeply, Socrates, but, apart from the communal activities which will be beneficial in themselves, I imagine that they would discuss various moral questions together, perhaps of a controversial and topical nature—for instance, questions about war and sexual behavior and the care of old people and so on."

"Yes, I thought that might be your answer. And you are not the only one to think along these lines, Antiphon. For already I see throughout our city many teachers who are doing this, whether in the 'school family' or in the classroom. They teach their pupils something they call 'social studies'—it has to do with the problems of our society, I imagine, and also they discuss moral problems of the topical kinds that you mention. This is sometimes described as 'religious education,' though I am not clear why."

"Well, and is this not a good thing?"

"No doubt it is, Antiphon. Certainly the teachers I speak of are extremely anxious to avoid imposing their own moral opinions on the pupils; they allow them to make up their minds for themselves. Indeed, some teachers I know will hardly say anything at all in the discussion, for fear of over-influencing the pupils. They act like the chairmen of committees, who do not advance any points themselves, but simply sum up the general opinion. Also, they are extremely diligent in providing, not only books, but also pictures and moving pictures and clippings from the newspapers and many other things that catch the eye easily."

"Are you being ironical again, Socrates?"

"Good heavens, no. I am sure that many pupils are stimulated, in a general sort of way, by such methods as these. They make a nice change, certainly, or indeed a kind of holiday, from their usual earnest studies of mathematics and science and other disciplines—though even these are, I believe, not so earnest as they used to be when I was a boy. However, one thing worries me."

"Well, what is that?"

"Are you familiar with signposts, Antiphon?"

"Of course."

"If you were a signpost at a crossroads, you would not point people down the wrong road, would you?"

"No; people would not attend to me for very long if I did that."

"But would it be much better if you pointed towards all the roads at once? I mean, if I wished to go to Thebes, and came to the crossroads, and you pointed down all four ways, that would not be very helpful, would it?"

"No, but I do not see the point of your parable."

"Then let me try a closer analogy, Antiphon. When we teach children science, we do not simply say to them: 'Children, there are certain facts which you must take for granted. We do not propose to give you the reasons for them, or allow you to question them—they are simply the truth, which you must accept from us,' and then proceed to tell them about the movements of the planets, and the tides, and light and heat, and so on, as if these were unquestionable truths. We do not act in that way, do we?"

"No, for we try to show them the reasons behind these truths (if they are such) and thereby to initiate them into the realm of science, so that they may think scientifically for themselves."

"But also, Antiphon, we do not say to them: 'Children, there are interesting questions about how the planets and tides move, and about the operation of heat and light and so forth. Now, we will let you discuss such questions, but we do not propose at all to show you how you may best find the answers for yourselves. Some people indeed, try to find the answers by making observations and conducting experiments, but others accept what Homer has said on such matters. Others again sit in armchairs and simply think about them, without observing at all—but we do not recommend any one of these methods more than another, for we are very anxious not to impose on you or indoctrinate you in such things.' We do not say that, do we?"

Pupils Need To Be Taught the Methodology of Morality

"No, for we know how to do the subject and can help children to adopt the right procedures."

"Just so, but do we not have something like the same knowledge in the case of morality?"

"Perhaps."

"I hope it is more than 'perhaps,' Antiphon. Otherwise all that we said earlier about the nature of moral reasons will have to be said again. If you remember, we said that such reasons had to be connected with human wants and needs—those of other people weighing equally with our own? Is that not what we said?"

"Oh, yes, of course."

"But can this not be taught to our pupils? And is it not important? For we can imagine, can we not, these pupils pleading piteously with us, even in the midst of all the books and materials and pictures which we give them, saying, 'O Antiphon, we are very grateful to you for providing us with this family group of friends and also for all these materials which arouse our interest, many of which we can use to decorate the walls of our rooms. But can you not help us further? Can you not show us how we ought to be thinking about these matters? We do not, of course, want you to tell us the answers, even if you know them; that would be like looking up the answer to a mathematical problem in the back of the textbook. But we would like to know what sort of reasons and procedures to use in deciding moral matters, for otherwise we feel lost and in a muddle.'"

"Well, I suppose we could teach them the difference between proper and improper reasons."

"Yes, indeed, and there must be many kinds of improper ones which they may be making use of because they know no better. For instance, they may simply quote some authority as a reason—'because I just felt it was right somehow'; or, again, their own advantage—'because it would pay me to do so.' In none of these cases would they be thinking about the interests of other people, as they ought to do."

"I think you have something there, Socrates. You mean that we should instruct our pupils openly and directly in moral reasoning?"

"Why not? And I would do more besides."

"What more?"

"Well, I remember that you and Cephalus very clearly outlined what was required for a good performance in the moral Olympics. Like those entering for the pentathlon or decathlon, they needed, not one thing only, but many different skills and abilities. We mentioned, did we not, the need for factual knowledge and knowledge of emotions and also the various powers of alertness and decision making and so on, which Cephalus talked about. If we are right about these—though no doubt they need further study and investigation—then ought we to lie to our pupils by keeping silent about them?"

"How do you mean, 'lie?'"

And Told What Equipment They Need

"I mean that we must tell them, frankly and honestly, that this is the equipment they need, and must use whenever they have a moral question to consider, and that, if they are going to be serious about the subject at all, they must try to cultivate these qualities in themselves (with the help of their teachers, of course). If we do not say this clearly to them, they could hardly help supposing, either that we had no idea of the necessary equipment, or that (for some sinister reason) we were concealing it from them—and in either case they would not trust us and would quite likely go off to some other trainer for their Olympics."

"Well, Socrates, I am bound to agree with you. But do you think that simply giving them this instruction will, in itself, bestow on them the qualities they need?"

"I didn't say that, Antiphon. But tell me, you are about to serve as a cavalry officer on the frontier, are you not?"

"Yes."

"Have you ever done such service before—indeed, are you familiar with horses and cavalry warfare?"

"Not at all."

"Yet I imagine that your instructor will think it worthwhile telling you something about them. He would agree, I think, that what he says will not necessarily make you a good cavalry officer, or even a good horseman; that comes with practice, and part of it may even be a matter of natural talent. But he will tell you what sorts of things you will need to learn: how to practice, how to look after your equipment, what sort of mistakes you may find yourself making, and so on. Will this not be very useful?"

"Yes, I see."

Morality Not Just Spread by Infection

"It seems to me, Antiphon, as if we may otherwise be in danger of behaving like the Britannicoi."

"And who are they?"

"They are a tribe of mad barbarians dwelling somewhere to the northwest, where it always rains. The belief there is that health is in some way caught, like disease, by infection or imitation. What they call 'the goodness of the body' (that is, health) they imagine to be transmitted in some magical way by other 'good' or healthy people. So they do not much mind what their children eat, or whether they take exercise, or whether they have learned to distinguish between suitable food and poisons, or understand about the way in which the body works—all they do is surround their children with 'good' or healthy people (a hard task, since as you may imagine, there are very few such) and expect that health will be transmitted to them in this way. When the children become ill or die, they say that this is because they had not been surrounded or infected by enough healthy people."

"How extraordinary!"

"Yes, but this is how many people in our own city think about virtue and morality. They do not perceive that it is a matter of giving our pupils many different things, but see it as the transmission of a single substance, which they call 'goodness' or 'moral virtue' or something of the kind—like the Britannicoi and health. That, in part, is why they are so slow to regard morality as something that can be studied as a serious subject, and (to some degree) taught like other subjects. To do this seems to them somehow blasphemous or degrading to morality."

"But surely, Socrates, you do not deny the importance of parents and teachers 'setting a good example,' as it is called?"

"I do not know whether to deny it or affirm it, Antiphon, since very little is known about the matter. Maybe it is very important, and like the force of example shown by a brave commander of hoplites. In this case, if you wish to get your men to charge, you will do best by charging yourself as bravely as possible; it is not much good reasoning with them. But it might also be like health, where the mere example of healthy people is not of much use. More likely, examples may be valuable for some aspects of morality but not for others. For it seems to me that we are still flirting with a mistress who is indeed attractive but who ought not properly to engage our affections."

"And which is she? Is she one of the imitation Virtues we were talking of?"

The Dangers of Doctrinaire Approaches

"No, but someone far more dangerous. Her name is Unity, and she would have us believe that morality is just one thing and that there must be one method of moral education only. She flourishes here as well as among the Britannicoi and has a technique of persuasion which is most effective."

"What does she say?"

"She does not even need to utter a complete sentence, Antiphon. She simply says, when any question about education (or anything else) is raised, 'Surely this is simply a matter of . . . ,'and leaves other people to finish it, which they do very eagerly. For instance, I have heard endings such as 'improving economic conditions,' 'overthrowing the capitalist system,' 'having teachers who really care for the children,' 'making education relevant to the modern world'—almost anything will do."

"That is very true, Socrates, and I must confess that when it comes to education I often despair of any clear thinking or drawing of distinctions at all. Perhaps it is that very few philosophers are concerned with the subject."

"Say rather, Antiphon, that very few people concerned with the subject are willing to philosophize. For philosophizing is not much more than an attempt to get clear. But now, at this time of night, I feel that I am more likely to obscure than to clarify if I go on talking; we had better continue tomorrow."

*   *   *

When I arrived in the morning I noticed that Cephalus looked rather pale, and so I said to him:

"Are you ill, Cephalus, or what? For I notice that you do not seem your usual self this morning."

"No Socrates, I am not. For I too have had a dream which was not at all pleasant."

"Of what kind?"

The Need for Scientific Research

"It was no lady Virtues that stood by my bed, but a number of severe old men, armed with measuring-rods and abacuses and curious machines that hummed and clicked. I thought at first that they might be demons from the underworld and that this was a false dream sent by Zeus, like the one he sent Agamemnon in Homer. But it turned out otherwise."

"But what did these severe old men want of you, Cephalus?"

"Well, one of them tapped me on the chest and spoke to me very fiercely, as follows: 'It is too bad of you, Cephalus! We expect that young men, like your son, Antiphon, will be rash and charge ahead without proper reflection, and as for Socrates—well, he is a philosopher and will no doubt say anything. But from older men like yourself we expect better treatment. Here you have been laying down the law about the use of many kinds of methods for instructing and improving the young as regards morality, but you have done no work to find out whether, in point of fact, these methods actually do what you claim for them. For all you know, they may do the opposite. You are like a lazy doctor who recommends certain herbs and medicines to a patient when he has never tried them out before or discovered as carefully as possible just what effects they have upon what sorts of people.'"

"And what did you reply?"

"I said nothing, but hung my head in shame, and he continued thus: 'No doubt it is amusing to speculate on these matters, Cephalus, and we don't blame you overmuch. But surely you will need to hire men like ourselves, who with the aid of our measuring-rods and machines, will help you to assess the effects of the methods you mention, and others besides. When we have worked with you for some time, we shall be able to tell you when the pupils become better or worse in respect of the various qualities you have outlined—the use of proper reasons and relevant knowledge and alertness and determination and all the rest. It will be a lengthy business, of course, but not until we have done this will you be able to recommend anything confidently.' And with that they vanished."

"By the gods, Cephalus, I think that they are right. They must be numbered among the experts we spoke of earlier—those whose business is not with concepts and ideas, as ours is, but who are skilled in measurement and the study of changes in the soul. Some of them, indeed, may not be completely trustworthy, but if we choose sensible ones and set a philosophical guard over them, as it were, I do believe that they will be of the greatest use to us."

"I suppose you are right, Socrates. But will Antiphon agree?"

And Hard Work

"I have thought so all along, father. For I have often noticed with older men like yourself and Socrates—if you will forgive me for saying so—that they seem to think that these problems can be tackled merely by thinking in armchairs, so to speak. And as Socrates has said, this sort of thinking may suit philosophy, but when we are called upon to determine the facts it will not do; it is likely to be no more than speculation or prejudice. Why, only the other day I heard people disputing on this point with quite unwarranted confidence. One said that all we needed to improve the morality of the young was to make them climb some high mountain, as it might be Pelion or Ossa, or to accustom them to sail together on triremes; while others advocated other methods, seeming to be equally certain about the merits of noble literature, or drama, or the beauties of nature. Yet it was clear to me that none of them had any real evidence for their views, nor, indeed, did they seem to think that evidence was in any way necessary."

"We are all to blame, Antiphon, not just Cephalus here. For it is always tempting to suppose that one knows, when in fact one does not know or anything like it. The methods we mentioned the other day—the ones concerned with setting up families, and the direct instruction in moral reasoning and other equipment for morality—may perhaps be satisfactory, but rather than inventing too many other methods which appeal to us, we shall do better to make a serious study of what actually happens in schools and other institutions. I am surprised that we did not notice this before."

"Well, but what are we to do in the meantime?"

Meanwhile We Must Be Clear About the General Aims

"Surely there is plenty of work for us, Antiphon. For I don't think that all those concerned with education—I don't mean only the teachers, but those who conduct the administration in our city, and those who are being trained to become teachers (if this is possible), and other people who have a general interest in the subject—I don't think, I say, that all these people are at all clear about the points which we three have worked out together. Yet, if they are not clear it is likely, is it not, that they will start off on quite the wrong foot. They will have false, dreamlike ideas about morality and about the moral equipment which the young need, and they will be likely to do all sorts of things in an attempt to influence them which may be useless or, indeed, positively harmful."

"Yes, but what can we do about it?"

"Well, Antiphon, we can try by every available method to clarify the position for these people. It will no doubt be a thankless task, since their dreams are so strong that they will prefer them to anything that we may say, at least in some cases. But it may be that, if we have patience the light will slowly dawn. I should not regard it as a waste of time if we tried as far as possible, to introduce, not only teachers, but all concerned with education to the philosophical aspects of the subject, for it is only then, I think, that they will have much hope of doing anything useful."

"Yes, I agree. but there is one other thing we can do—or, at least, have done for us."

"What is that?"

"These experts that you spoke of, Socrates—I mean

those who have made a study of the individual soul and how it develops in groups of people and in the city generally—may not, perhaps, have spent much of their time considering morality, but surely they will have things to tell us of a general kind, which will be relevant to our own interests."

The Importance of Psychology

"How do you mean, Antiphon?"

"Well, for instance, there are many doctors of the mind who for a long time now have been engaged in studying the individual soul, from the age of infancy onwards. They spend much effort in trying to assist those whose minds have become ill in various ways, and probably they know more about certain aspects of the mind than most other people. It is true that they are not specifically concerned with morality—or at least, they do not use that word very much. But they will be able to tell us in general how children develop as they grow older and what things there are which are necessary for a healthy development—I mean, as regards discipline and affection and the influence of parents and so on. Surely it is important for us, and for the teachers, to know what they have said. Indeed, my idea about setting up families in the school and creating conditions in which there may be trust and affection between pupils and teachers was borrowed from what I have read in the works of these doctors. This is only one example, Socrates, of the ways in which experts can help us."

"Have you others?"

"Certainly, if you wish to hear them. I will mention just one, however. There is a person who lectures in the academy about what he calls 'nonverbal communication' and 'social skills,' which. . . ."

"Please translate that into ordinary Greek, Antiphon, otherwise I shall not understand you."

"Well, the idea is that people affect each other, not only by what they say, but by such things as the expressions on their faces, and their bodily postures, and things of that kind. Indeed, as he claims, these things are much more forceful and effective in the dealings men have with each other than the actual words which they use. So that it might be possible to train teachers—and perhaps pupils— in these skills, for obviously they would be very relevant to satisfying other people's interests, which we have seen to be the cornerstone of morality."

"How interesting, Antiphon. I had no idea that this work was going on, though I see, now you mention it, that it has great importance for us."

"Yes, and there are many other things of the same sort. For this is a vast subject that we have undertaken, Socrates."

Morality Not Only Relevant to Schools

"It is indeed; bigger than we have yet considered, perhaps."

"What, bigger still?"

"Yes, for hitherto we have confined our discussion to schools, that being the most obvious place for moral education to be conducted. But tell me, you do not only speak when you are have elocution lessons, do you?"

"Of course not."

"Or run only when you are entered for the Olympics, or in training for them?"

"No."

"In just the same way, Antiphon, there will be other places and times, besides those that occur in schools, which are important for the morality of our young people. Indeed, we considered one of them when you related the dialogue you had with Adeimantus—I mean, the effect on the young of viewing certain spectacles and reading certain literature: For this, you know, hardly happens at all in school, but outside it."

"True, but by this argument, there will be few places and times that do not in one way or another affect the moral development of a person. For it will make a difference what sort of family he has, and how he spends his holidays away from school; what his friends are like, and what work he does; what sort of city he lives in, and what its laws and customs are like—all these and more will be relevant. Moreover—something I have only just thought of—it is not the case that we are exclusively interested in the young, is it?"

"How do you mean, Antiphon?"

Nor Only to the Young

"I mean that older people also have much to learn about morality, and they need this knowledge just as much, or more, than young people. Presumably you do not imagine that a person will know all he needs to know by the time he is adult?"

"Not at all; there is an infinite amount to learn."

"So then this sort of education will continue throughout life—or ought to do so."

"Yes, you are right. Yet how few people try to continue their education after they leave school or the academy! For the most part, I think, they seem only too glad to have escaped from such institutions, regarding them (it seems) as not much better than prisons."

"I suppose this is just one more indication of how unwilling people are to learn anything, Socrates. For when they are adult and no longer under any kind of compulsion they spend their time in making money and other such things, buying what they enjoy (or think they enjoy) and indulging in various kinds of pleasures—travel and the like—what they imagine will make them happy. And yet, for the most part, they do not seem very happy to me."

"Very true, Antiphon. I think Cephalus was right when he said that there were two big things, love and work, which made men happy, and not these other things at all. But do you see what is happening?"

"What?"

"Since we have agreed to investigate the value of our educational methods more scientifically, using whatever experts we can find, we have allowed our discussion to wither away, like a plant from lack of water. We are, in effect, admitting, not so much that we have no further problems to discuss, for that is far from the case, but that there is not much point in discussing them except in the company of these other experts. And this is all the more true in that, as we have just seen, our range of activities is extremely wide. We are interested, not only in schools, but in families and cities and everything else besides. So I suggest, then, that for the time being at least we bring our discussions to a close. Do you agree, Cephalus?"

"Yes, Socrates, but there is one more matter, to conclude the banquet of our discussion, which I should like to tell you about; perhaps you will allow me time to do so after dinner. Then I shall be quite happy to let you go and reflect for some time on what we have learned."

"Very well, Cephalus; let us meet for the last time after dinner."

CHAPTER 7

Conclusion

When dinner was over, I saw that Cephalus appeared slightly nervous (despite all the wine that had been drunk), so I spoke to him encouragingly, saying:

Cephalus' Original Plan

"Come on, Cephalus! We shall not be seeing each other for some time now, and if there is something you would like to say, please do so confidently. After all, this is your house, and after such an excellent dinner how could we deny you anything? Indeed, if you remember, it was you who put us on the track of this whole discussion in the first place. Do you recall, on our first day, how I found you lamenting Antiphon's behavior, and how this led us to consider all these problems that we have talked of?"

"It is just that, Socrates, which I wanted to speak about. I am not a clever man, I know, but I want to do my best and to behave generously, and I am anxious not to make a fool of myself twice."

"I did not think you foolish then, Cephalus, nor shall I think so now. But tell me, what is in your mind?"

"Well, Socrates, if you recall our first discussion, I said that I was going to assemble a group of 'right-minded, thoroughly respectable' men and promote the moral education of young people with their help, on the basis of religion. They were to help me collect the writings of the 'good sages,' and in general promote what was decent and honorable and noble, as it then seemed to me. These men were not to be either philosophers, such as yourself, nor the experts that we talked about recently, but older men who had been honored by the state and seemed to share my ideas."

He Sees It Now as a Fantasy

"Yes, I remember that. But how do you now feel about your plan?"

"The truth is, Socrates, that I am only just beginning to understand my own motives. For you must know (and this, I fear, I have concealed from you) that I was persuaded some time ago to give some money to a group of philosophers and experts at the academy to investigate this subject. Indeed I gave quite a lot of money, for about six or seven years."

"And what happened?"

"Well, I had not then the benefit of your conversation, Socrates, and I was, I think, somewhat more ignorant and in a dream (as you would say) than perhaps I am now. As time went on, these philosophers and experts at the academy produced various writings about morality and religion, many of which I did not understand—though I see now that some of them were like what we ourselves have just been saying. This baffled and alarmed me, and I felt that I was not getting what I paid for. I had hoped, I suppose, that these experts would produce some simple stuff which would bolster up my own dreams and prejudices for me and enable me to extend my fantasies into the real world."

"Yes, I understand. Of course, you were at a disadvantage because of your wealth."

"How so, Socrates?"

"The wealthy are accustomed, are they not, to order the world very much as they choose. I mean, they can employ and dismiss whom they will and do not have to attend to the opinions and desires of anyone, so long as they remain within the law. Indeed, it is difficult for a wealthy man in this position to get an honest opinion at all—particularly if he is as pleasant a person as you are, Cephalus. Most people will naturally defer to him and try to keep him happy, either out of natural goodness or because they are prudent and know which side their bread is buttered on. Perhaps you regarded these philosophers and experts, not as equal allies whose opinions you felt you had to respect, but rather as gardeners or maidservants whom you hired simply in order to carry out your will."

"I am ashamed to say that you may be right, Socrates. For certainly I did not trust them to do the work in their own way. So, after I had kept quiet (though with mounting concern) for a number of years, I disbanded most of them and started to consider the other plan—I mean, the one about gathering a group of respectable men who would help me to disseminate the 'good sages.' Indeed, I suppose that I had hoped that this is what the experts at the academy would do in the first place, though, now that I reflect, the hope was absurd."

"Well, then, Cephalus, how do you stand now?"

"It looks as if I shall have to admit to having made a mistake, Socrates, in disbanding the group of academy experts in the first place. And I was on the verge of another mistake in my second plan. For, as it now seems to me, the 'respectable men' I wanted to collect were really not those who were best qualified to investigate this difficult topic."

"On what basis did you select them, then?"

"I suppose I wanted people as much like myself as possible, only better and more honorable—like elder brothers or fathers who agreed with my own opinions. Perhaps what I really had in mind was not a team of experts to find out what we did not know. If I had wanted that, I should probably have stuck to the academy experts. What I really wanted, I think, was a kind of club or dining-party of like-minded men who could keep each other and myself happy by constantly expressing the same opinions."

And a Kind of Selfishness

"Well, there is no reason why you should not establish such a thing, Cephalus; after all, you can do what you like with your own money."

"Yes, Socrates, but now I am somewhat disenchanted with the idea. For this seems to be not much more than an extension of my own dream of a group of people who find security in dreaming together, as certain religious sects who believe fantastic doctrines find comfort in sharing them with each other. They are not concerned to examine whether the doctrines are true. Indeed, they are not interested in thinking and arguing and cross-questioning at all. I feel, also, that in a way I have not been as generous as I supposed."

"How? Surely you have spent a great deal of money unselfishly."

"I am not sure about the 'unselfishly,' Socrates. I seem to myself like a rich father who will not give his children money to do what they like with, but who always give it 'with strings attached,' as they say. Such a man is interested in implementing his own desires, not in the good of other men."

"I think you are a little too harsh with yourself, Cephalus. You supposed at the time that your own desires and dreams were to be identified with the good of others—in effect, that the 'good sages' whom you favored were bound to be 'good' for young people and others as well. On that assumption, you were justified in what you did. All that has happened, isn't it, is that you have begun to question the assumption."

"And a very painful questioning it has been, Socrates, if I may say so—even though you have handled me very gently."

"Well, Cephalus, 'learning by suffering' is the law for us poor mortals, as Aeschylus says. If philosophy does not hurt, it is not of much use. Remember what we said about men fearing the light because it dazzles them and is painful. But you are not like the majority of men, who will not open their eyes at all; if you had been—to speak frankly— it would have been a waste of time conversing with you. Not that I think that I know better than you—that is far from the case—but rather that, if you had not been willing to discuss and argue and take account of opinions opposite to your own (rather that just shouting them down), this conversation would not have been possible."

His Changed Ideas

"You encourage me, Socrates. But now I must consider how best to spend my money, for if what we said is true about the duty of satisfying the interests of others, I should not consider it my own money in any absolute sense, but rather spend it in the general interest, not only for myself. Can you not give me some advice about how to do this?"

"I should not wish to advise you in general, Cephalus. But if you are still concerned with moral education and the improvement of the young, we have already agreed among ourselves what sort of work is necessary."

"True, Socrates, and I should, I think, like to devote some part of my resources to that work. For the other day I happened to be reading of the various ways in which rich men had spent their money. Some of them built crazy buildings-'follies,' I think they are called. Others promoted various enterprises which appealed to their whims and prejudices. In general what they did was stupid and the result is that they have left no name behind them, except a name for stupidity and willfullness. I want to do rather better than that. What now seems to me important is, not what I myself am keen on in the sense of being naturally prejudiced in its favor, but what actually needs to be done."

"That seems to me a great step forward, Cephalus, and I am very glad you have taken it. For I must tell you that I have always had a great affection for you, besides feeling much gratitude for all the entertainment and hospitality you have afforded me, and I am glad to have been of some small service."

"Not small, Socrates, but great, and I am sure that Antiphon will agree with me. But now the day is drawing to a close—as our lives are, indeed. Yet I still have hopes that we shall be able to achieve some important thing which will be of real benefit to future generations. Farewell, Socrates, for the time being. I am sure, though, that within a very short time I shall want to apply to you again for advice."

"I never give advice, Cephalus, except to those who are willing to receive it. But since I see that you are more willing than you were, I hope to be of help to you. Farewell."

Index